CALEB ROSS

ASP.NET Core MVC with Angular For Beginners

Copyright © 2024 by Caleb Ross

All rights reserved. No part of this publication may be reproduced, stored or transmitted in any form or by any means, electronic, mechanical, photocopying, recording, scanning, or otherwise without written permission from the publisher. It is illegal to copy this book, post it to a website, or distribute it by any other means without permission.

First edition

This book was professionally typeset on Reedsy.
Find out more at reedsy.com

Contents

Introduction	1
Chapter 1: Getting Started with ASP.NET Core and Angular	9
Chapter 2: Understanding MVC Architecture in ASP.NET Core	22
Chapter 3: Angular Fundamentals	38
Chapter 4: Building Your First Full-Stack Application	54
Chapter 5: Working with Data and Databases	74
Chapter 6: Implementing Authentication and Authorization in...	90
Chapter 7: Error Handling and Validation in Your Full-Stack...	114
Chapter 8: Enhancing User Experience with UI/UX Design...	125
Chapter 9: Performance Optimization Techniques for...	136
Chapter 10: Deploying Your Full-Stack Application	150
Chapter 11: Security Best Practices for Full-Stack...	164
Chapter 12: Continuous Improvement and Future Enhancements	173
Chapter 13: Community and Support in Application Development	183
Chapter 13: Deployment Strategies and Best Practices for...	191
Chapter 14: Final Thoughts and the Future of Your Full-Stack...	206
Chapter 15: Navigating the Future of Full-Stack Development	214
Conclusion: Charting Your Path in Full-Stack Development	223

Introduction

Overview of ASP.NET Core MVC and Angular

In the current landscape of web development, full-stack proficiency has become increasingly valuable. Two key technologies dominating the web development sphere are ASP.NET Core MVC (Model-View-Controller) and Angular. Both frameworks offer powerful capabilities that streamline the development process for both back-end and front-end development.

ASP.NET Core MVC is a web application framework developed by Microsoft, designed to build dynamic, data-driven websites and web applications. As a successor to the older ASP.NET framework, ASP.NET Core is faster, more efficient, and cross-platform, allowing developers to create applications that can run on Windows, macOS, and Linux. The MVC pattern helps separate the application logic into three interconnected components: the model (handling data logic), the view (managing the user interface), and the controller (processing user requests and input). This separation of concerns promotes organized, scalable, and maintainable code.

On the other side of the stack, **Angular**, a front-end web application framework developed by Google, is designed to create dynamic and responsive user interfaces. Angular is component-based, which means that the application's UI is divided into independent, reusable pieces called components. Angular's declarative approach to UI development and its powerful data-binding capabilities make it one of the most preferred frameworks for building modern, single-page applications (SPAs). It is based on TypeScript, a superset of JavaScript, which adds static types to your code and helps catch errors early during development.

The combination of ASP.NET Core MVC and Angular offers developers a full-stack framework for building web applications from the ground up. ASP.NET Core handles the server-side logic, manages database interactions, and provides the necessary APIs for the front-end to consume. Angular, on the other hand, manages the client-side, ensuring that the user interface is responsive, interactive, and visually appealing.

This book is designed to help you master both of these powerful frameworks, providing you with the knowledge needed to build full-stack applications that can scale and perform at enterprise-level standards. Throughout this book, you will learn how to seamlessly integrate ASP.NET Core MVC with Angular, building modern applications that provide an excellent user experience, perform efficiently, and are easy to maintain.

Why Full-Stack Development Matters

In today's fast-paced digital age, businesses and organizations demand more sophisticated, scalable, and responsive web applications. Whether it's an e-commerce platform, a content management system, or a data-driven enterprise portal, users expect high-quality, interactive, and seamless experiences. This shift in expectations has given rise to the importance of **full-stack development.**

Full-stack development refers to the ability to work on both the front-end and back-end of a web application. Full-stack developers are proficient in both server-side technologies (back-end) and client-side technologies (front-end). While specialization in either back-end or front-end development is valuable, full-stack developers can bridge the gap between the two, understanding how the entire application operates as a cohesive unit.

Here's why full-stack development matters in the current web development ecosystem:

1. **Improved Efficiency and Flexibility**: Full-stack developers can work on both ends of the development pipeline, allowing for smoother

communication and integration between the front-end and back-end of the application. This leads to faster development cycles and easier troubleshooting since a full-stack developer can navigate both aspects of the application.
2. **Cost-Effective**: In a world where startups and enterprises are constantly seeking ways to optimize costs, full-stack developers are valuable assets. With the ability to work across the entire stack, full-stack developers reduce the need for multiple specialists, making them highly sought-after by companies that need to do more with fewer resources.
3. **Seamless Integration**: Full-stack developers have a holistic understanding of the entire web development process, allowing them to better integrate front-end and back-end functionalities. They can write APIs and immediately consume them on the client side, making integration between different parts of an application smoother and less error-prone.
4. **Cross-Platform Capabilities**: With technologies like ASP.NET Core MVC being cross-platform, full-stack developers are empowered to create applications that can run on various operating systems and devices. This versatility ensures that businesses can reach their users no matter what platform they are on.
5. **Better Troubleshooting**: Having the ability to understand both the client-side and server-side aspects of an application enables full-stack developers to diagnose and fix issues faster. They can see the full picture, from how the data flows from the server to the browser, making them more effective problem solvers.
6. **Career Advancement**: Full-stack development skills are in high demand. By mastering both back-end and front-end technologies, developers position themselves as versatile professionals who can adapt to various roles, making them attractive candidates for a wide range of development positions.

In the context of this book, mastering **ASP.NET Core MVC** and **Angular** provides you with the tools necessary to excel in full-stack development. ASP.NET Core MVC takes care of the back-end logic, managing data storage, handling HTTP requests, and serving up RESTful APIs. Angular, on the other hand, handles the user interface, providing a dynamic and smooth user experience. Together, these two technologies form the foundation for building modern, robust, and scalable web applications.

What You Will Learn in This Book

This book is structured to take you from a beginner to a proficient full-stack developer by focusing on ASP.NET Core MVC and Angular. By the end of this book, you will have gained a deep understanding of how to create full-stack applications that handle data management, user interaction, and performance optimization.

Here's a breakdown of what you will learn:

1. **Setting Up Your Development Environment**: From installing .NET Core SDK, Visual Studio, Node.js, and Angular CLI to creating your first ASP.NET Core and Angular projects, you'll start with a strong foundation in both back-end and front-end development.
2. **Understanding MVC Architecture**: You'll learn how the Model-View-Controller pattern works in ASP.NET Core, how to structure your application logically, and how to build your first web application using this pattern.
3. **Angular Fundamentals**: You'll dive deep into Angular, learning about its core components such as modules, components, services, and directives. You'll also learn how data binding, routing, and state management are handled in Angular.
4. **Full-Stack Integration**: You'll discover how to seamlessly integrate ASP.NET Core MVC with Angular to build a fully functional web application. From routing to data exchange between front-end and back-end, you'll understand how these two technologies complement each other.
5. **Building RESTful APIs with ASP.NET Core**: You'll learn how to create, read, update, and delete data using ASP.NET Core Web APIs, and how to consume these APIs in Angular applications.
6. **Data Management and Entity Framework Core**: You'll learn how to

INTRODUCTION

manage data using Entity Framework Core, create models, and interact with databases efficiently.

7. **User Authentication and Authorization**: Security is a crucial part of web applications. You'll learn how to implement user authentication using ASP.NET Core Identity and secure your application with role-based access control.
8. **State Management and RxJS in Angular**: You'll explore how to manage the state of your Angular application using services, observables, and RxJS. You'll also learn advanced state management using NgRx.
9. **Forms, Validation, and Error Handling**: You'll master handling forms and implementing client-side and server-side validation in Angular. You'll also learn how to manage errors effectively, providing a smooth user experience.
10. **Testing and Debugging**: You'll gain insight into testing your code, including unit testing for ASP.NET Core and Angular. Debugging tools and techniques will also be covered to help you troubleshoot common issues.
11. **Deploying and Hosting Applications**: You'll learn how to prepare your application for production, deploy it on web servers like IIS, and host it on cloud platforms like Azure.
12. **Best Practices and Optimization**: Finally, you'll learn best practices for writing clean, maintainable code and how to optimize your full-stack applications for performance and scalability.

Who Is This Book For?

This book is tailored for individuals who are new to full-stack development or have some experience in web development but want to expand their skills. Here's a breakdown of the target audience:

1. **Beginners to Web Development**: If you're just starting your journey into web development, this book will provide you with a solid foundation in both back-end and front-end development. It is written in a way that even those with little programming experience will find approachable.

2. **Front-End Developers**: If you already have experience working with front-end technologies such as HTML, CSS, and JavaScript, but you want to understand how to build and integrate a powerful back-end with ASP.NET Core MVC, this book is perfect for you.
3. **Back-End Developers**: For those who are already familiar with server-side development using technologies like ASP.NET or other back-end languages, this book will teach you how to implement a modern front-end using Angular.
4. **Full-Stack Developers**: If you're already a full-stack developer but want to add ASP.NET Core MVC and Angular to your toolkit, this book will provide you with detailed insights into how these technologies work together to create robust applications.
5. **Students and Educators**: This book can be a valuable resource for students learning about full-stack development and for educators who want to use it as a reference material in courses related to web development.
6. **Software Engineers Looking to Modernize Their Skills**: As the demand for modern, responsive web applications continues to grow, this book provides software engineers with the knowledge they need to stay competitive in the job market by learning the latest technologies in ASP.NET Core and Angular.

Tools and Environment Setup

Before diving into the technical aspects of ASP.NET Core MVC and Angular, it's important to set up your development environment correctly. Ensuring you have the right tools will streamline your development process and help you avoid common setup issues.

1. .NET Core SDK

To build applications using ASP.NET Core MVC, you need to install the .NET Core SDK. This software development kit provides the necessary tools and libraries to develop and run .NET applications across different platforms. You can download the SDK from the official .NET website.

Once installed, you can verify the installation by running the following command in your terminal:

```css
Copy code
dotnet --version
```

This should output the version of the SDK that has been installed.

2. Visual Studio (or Visual Studio Code)

Visual Studio is an Integrated Development Environment (IDE) developed by Microsoft, and it's the most commonly used tool for developing .NET applications. While Visual Studio offers a full-featured IDE experience, **Visual Studio Code** is a lightweight, cross-platform code editor that can be used with extensions for .NET and Angular development.

For beginners, Visual Studio Community Edition (free) is a great starting point. You can download it from the Visual Studio website.

3. Node.js and Angular CLI

To develop Angular applications, you'll need to install Node.js, which allows you to run JavaScript code outside the browser. It also includes the Node Package Manager (npm), which is essential for installing Angular CLI and other dependencies.

Download Node.js from Node.js official website.

Once Node.js is installed, you can install the Angular CLI globally by running the following command in your terminal:

```bash
Copy code
npm install -g @angular/cli
```

Verify the installation by running:

```css
Copy code
```

```
ng --version
```

4. SQL Server (or any other database)

For data storage and management, you'll need a relational database. **SQL Server** is commonly used with ASP.NET Core applications, but you can also use other databases such as MySQL or PostgreSQL. SQL Server Express Edition is a free version that is perfect for development purposes.

Download SQL Server Express from the Microsoft website.

5. Git and GitHub (Optional but Recommended)

Version control is a crucial part of any development process. Git is the most popular version control system, and GitHub is a platform where you can host and share your repositories. While optional, using Git will allow you to track changes to your code, collaborate with others, and deploy your application easily.

Download Git from the Git website.

6. Docker (Optional but Recommended)

For those interested in containerizing their applications for easy deployment, **Docker** is a powerful tool that allows you to package your application with all its dependencies into a container. This ensures that your application runs the same way regardless of the environment.

Download Docker from the Docker website.

7. Postman (Optional for API Testing)

Testing your APIs is crucial during development. **Postman** is a powerful tool that allows you to send HTTP requests to your APIs and inspect the responses. It's extremely useful for ensuring that your back-end is working as expected before integrating it with the Angular front-end.

Download Postman from the Postman website.

Chapter 1: Getting Started with ASP.NET Core and Angular

Introduction to ASP.NET Core MVC and Angular Frameworks

Before diving into the technical setup and the process of building a full-stack application, it's essential to understand what ASP.NET Core MVC and Angular bring to the table. Together, they provide a powerful combination for creating modern web applications that are robust, scalable, and efficient. This chapter will introduce you to these two frameworks, guide you through setting up the development environment, and help you build your first ASP.NET Core MVC and Angular applications.

ASP.NET Core MVC Overview

ASP.NET Core MVC is an open-source web application framework developed by Microsoft. It is a lightweight, cross-platform version of the ASP.NET framework and provides tools to build dynamic web applications that can scale from small projects to enterprise-level applications.

One of the key features of ASP.NET Core is its adherence to the **Model-View-Controller (MVC)** design pattern. The MVC pattern separates the application's logic into three interconnected components:

1. **Model**: Manages the data logic. The model represents the data and the rules that govern the manipulation of that data. In web development,

the model is typically responsible for handling the interaction with databases or external APIs.
2. **View**: Manages the user interface logic. The view is responsible for rendering the user interface based on the data received from the model. This includes the HTML, CSS, and JavaScript that are presented to the user.
3. **Controller**: Handles user input and requests. The controller acts as an intermediary between the model and the view. It processes user requests, manipulates the data via the model, and then returns the appropriate view to the user.

Why Use ASP.NET Core MVC?

- **Cross-platform**: ASP.NET Core can run on Windows, macOS, and Linux, allowing developers to build applications for any platform.
- **Modular and Lightweight**: ASP.NET Core is highly modular, allowing developers to include only the libraries and dependencies they need.
- **Performance**: ASP.NET Core is optimized for performance, making it one of the fastest web application frameworks available.
- **Security**: Built-in security features like authentication, authorization, and data protection make it easier to build secure web applications.
- **Integration with Modern Front-End Frameworks**: ASP.NET Core MVC works seamlessly with modern front-end frameworks like Angular, React, and Vue.js.

Angular Overview

Angular, developed by Google, is one of the most popular front-end frameworks used for building dynamic single-page applications (SPAs). It allows developers to create fast, interactive, and responsive user interfaces. Angular is built on **TypeScript**, a statically typed superset of JavaScript that adds features like types and interfaces, making the code more robust and easier to maintain.

Some of the key features of Angular include:

1. **Component-Based Architecture**: Angular uses components to build the UI. A component is a self-contained unit that includes HTML, CSS, and JavaScript (or TypeScript). Each component controls a part of the view and can be reused throughout the application.
2. **Two-Way Data Binding**: Angular provides two-way data binding, which allows the synchronization of data between the model and the view. This ensures that any changes made in the user interface are immediately reflected in the application's data, and vice versa.
3. **Dependency Injection**: Angular has a built-in dependency injection system that allows components to share services and other resources, making it easier to manage the application's dependencies.
4. **Routing**: Angular comes with a powerful routing module that allows developers to define routes and manage navigation between different views of the application.
5. **Directives**: Angular uses directives to extend the capabilities of HTML. Directives allow you to attach behavior to DOM elements, making it easier to build dynamic and reusable components.

Why Use Angular?

- **Single Page Applications (SPA)**: Angular is designed for building SPAs, where the entire application runs within a single web page and dynamically updates as users interact with it.
- **Declarative UI**: Angular allows developers to declare how the UI should look based on the state of the data, reducing the need to manipulate the DOM directly.
- **Strong Community Support**: As one of the most widely used front-end frameworks, Angular has a large community and ecosystem, which makes it easier to find resources, libraries, and solutions to common problems.
- **Cross-Platform Development**: Angular can be used to build web, mobile, and desktop applications, providing flexibility across different platforms.

Combining ASP.NET Core MVC and Angular

The combination of ASP.NET Core MVC and Angular allows developers to create **full-stack web applications**. ASP.NET Core takes care of the server-side logic, such as interacting with the database and managing authentication, while Angular handles the client-side logic, rendering the user interface and managing user interactions.

Using ASP.NET Core and Angular together offers several benefits:

- **Separation of Concerns**: The back-end and front-end codebases are kept separate, making the application easier to maintain and scale.
- **Faster Development**: Both frameworks offer tools and features that speed up development, such as scaffolding in ASP.NET Core and the Angular CLI.
- **Performance**: Angular SPAs load faster because only the required data is fetched from the server, reducing the overall bandwidth usage and improving performance.

In the following sections, we'll guide you through setting up your development environment and creating your first ASP.NET Core MVC and Angular applications.

Setting Up the Development Environment

Before you can start building web applications with ASP.NET Core and Angular, you need to set up your development environment. This includes installing the necessary tools, such as Visual Studio, Node.js, and Angular CLI. Here's a step-by-step guide to setting up the environment on your machine.

1. Visual Studio

Visual Studio is an Integrated Development Environment (IDE) developed by Microsoft. It provides all the tools needed to build ASP.NET Core applications, including project templates, code editors, debuggers, and more.

- **Installing Visual Studio**:

CHAPTER 1: GETTING STARTED WITH ASP.NET CORE AND ANGULAR

1. Download the Visual Studio installer from the official website.
2. Run the installer and select the **ASP.NET and web development** workload. This will install all the necessary components for ASP.NET Core development.
3. Once the installation is complete, launch Visual Studio and sign in with your Microsoft account.

- **Visual Studio Code (Alternative)**: If you prefer a lightweight editor, you can use **Visual Studio Code** (VS Code), which is a free and open-source code editor developed by Microsoft. VS Code is highly customizable and supports various extensions for both ASP.NET Core and Angular development.

To install VS Code, visit the official website and download the appropriate version for your operating system.

2. .NET Core SDK

The .NET Core SDK (Software Development Kit) is required to build and run ASP.NET Core applications. The SDK includes the necessary libraries, tools, and runtime to develop .NET applications.

- **Installing .NET Core SDK**:

1. Download the latest version of the .NET Core SDK from the official .NET website.
2. Run the installer and follow the on-screen instructions to complete the installation.
3. After installation, verify that the SDK is installed by opening a terminal or command prompt and typing the following command:

```css
Copy code
```

```
dotnet --version
```

- This command should return the version number of the installed SDK.
- **Visual Studio Integration**: If you're using Visual Studio, the installer will automatically include the .NET Core SDK as part of the ASP.NET workload. You can start creating ASP.NET Core projects directly within Visual Studio.

3. Node.js and npm (Node Package Manager)

Node.js is a JavaScript runtime that allows you to run JavaScript code outside of the browser. It's essential for Angular development because Angular's build process relies on Node.js and npm (Node Package Manager).

- **Installing Node.js**:

1. Download the latest stable version of Node.js from the official website.
2. Run the installer and follow the instructions.
3. After installation, verify that Node.js and npm are installed by running the following commands in a terminal or command prompt:

```css
Copy code
node --version
npm --version
```

- This should return the version numbers of Node.js and npm, indicating successful installation.

4. Angular CLI (Command Line Interface)

Angular CLI is a powerful tool that simplifies Angular development. It allows you to scaffold new projects, generate components, services, and

CHAPTER 1: GETTING STARTED WITH ASP.NET CORE AND ANGULAR

modules, and handle the build and deployment process.

- **Installing Angular CLI**: Once Node.js and npm are installed, you can install Angular CLI globally using npm. Open a terminal or command prompt and run the following command:

```bash
Copy code
npm install -g @angular/cli
```

- This will install Angular CLI globally on your system. You can verify the installation by running:

```css
Copy code
ng --version
```

- This should display the version of Angular CLI installed.

With these tools installed, your development environment is now ready for building ASP.NET Core MVC and Angular applications. In the following sections, we'll guide you through creating your first ASP.NET Core MVC project and Angular app.

Installing .NET Core SDK

As previously mentioned, the .NET Core SDK is essential for developing ASP.NET Core applications. The SDK includes the tools required to build, debug, and run your applications. Let's take a deeper dive into what the SDK offers and how to get it set up on your machine.

What is the .NET Core SDK?

The .NET Core SDK provides everything needed to create, build, and run .NET Core applications. It includes the following components:

- **.NET Core CLI (Command-Line Interface)**: A set of cross-platform tools for building and running .NET applications from the command line.
- **.NET Core Runtime**: The runtime that executes .NET Core applications. It includes the libraries and components required to run .NET Core apps.
- **ASP.NET Core Libraries**: A collection of libraries that enable the development of web applications using ASP.NET Core.

Step-by-Step Installation of .NET Core SDK

1. **Download the SDK**: Go to the official .NET website and download the latest version of the .NET Core SDK for your operating system (Windows, macOS, or Linux).
2. **Run the Installer**: Once the download is complete, run the installer and follow the on-screen instructions. The installer will automatically configure the necessary environment variables, such as adding the dotnet command to your system's PATH.
3. **Verify the Installation**: After the installation is complete, open a terminal or command prompt and type the following command:

```css
Copy code
dotnet --version
```

1. This command should return the installed SDK version. If you see a version number, the SDK has been installed successfully.

CHAPTER 1: GETTING STARTED WITH ASP.NET CORE AND ANGULAR

2. **Creating a Sample .NET Core Application**: You can test the installation by creating a simple console application. In the terminal or command prompt, navigate to a directory where you want to store the project, and run the following commands:

```arduino
Copy code
dotnet new console -o MyFirstApp
cd MyFirstApp
dotnet run
```

1. This will create a new console application, navigate to the project directory, and run the application. You should see the output "Hello World!" in the terminal, confirming that the SDK is installed and functioning correctly.

Creating Your First ASP.NET Core MVC Project

Now that you have the .NET Core SDK and Visual Studio installed, it's time to create your first ASP.NET Core MVC project. We'll walk you through the process of setting up a basic web application using ASP.NET Core MVC in Visual Studio.

Step-by-Step Guide to Creating an ASP.NET Core MVC Project

1. **Open Visual Studio**: Launch Visual Studio from your desktop or start menu.
2. **Create a New Project**: In the Visual Studio welcome screen, click on "**Create a new project**". This will open a project template selection screen.
3. **Select ASP.NET Core Web Application**: From the list of available templates, select "**ASP.NET Core Web Application**" and click **Next**. Name your project (for example, "MyFirstMVCApp") and choose a

location on your machine to save it.
4. **Configure the Project**: In the next screen, select **ASP.NET Core 5.0** or later as the target framework. Under the project type, select **Web Application (Model-View-Controller)** to create a project with the MVC design pattern. Click **Create** to generate the project.
5. **Explore the Project Structure**: Once the project is created, Visual Studio will generate a default ASP.NET Core MVC project structure. Here's an overview of the key components:

- **Controllers**: This folder contains the controller classes, which handle incoming HTTP requests and return responses.
- **Views**: This folder contains the HTML files, or Razor Views, that render the user interface.
- **Models**: This folder is where you define the data models for your application, which represent the data stored in your database.
- **wwwroot**: This folder contains static files, such as CSS, JavaScript, and images.

1. **Run the Project**: Press **F5** or click on the **Run** button in Visual Studio to start the application. This will launch the project in your default browser, and you should see a basic homepage with the text "Welcome."

Congratulations! You've just created your first ASP.NET Core MVC application. In the next section, we'll explore Angular and set up a basic Angular project.

Introduction to Angular CLI and Creating Angular App

The Angular CLI (Command Line Interface) is a powerful tool that simplifies Angular development. It provides commands to scaffold new projects, generate components, services, and modules, and handle the build and deployment process. In this section, we'll explore the Angular CLI and create our first Angular application.

CHAPTER 1: GETTING STARTED WITH ASP.NET CORE AND ANGULAR

What is Angular CLI?

The Angular CLI is a command-line tool designed to automate common tasks in Angular development. It helps developers avoid boilerplate code and provides a streamlined way to create and manage Angular projects.

Here are some of the features of Angular CLI:

- **Project Scaffolding**: Quickly generate new Angular projects with the ng new command.
- **Code Generation**: Use commands like ng generate to create components, services, modules, pipes, and more.
- **Development Server**: Use the ng serve command to launch a development server with live-reload capabilities.
- **Testing**: Easily set up and run unit tests and end-to-end tests for your Angular application using ng test and ng e2e.
- **Build and Deployment**: Use the ng build command to bundle your Angular app for production, optimizing the code for performance.

Setting Up Angular CLI

If you haven't already installed Angular CLI, follow these steps to set it up:

1. **Install Node.js**: Angular CLI requires Node.js, which you should have already installed in the previous steps.
2. **Install Angular CLI**: Open a terminal or command prompt and run the following command to install Angular CLI globally:

```bash
Copy code
npm install -g @angular/cli
```

1. **Verify Installation**: After the installation is complete, verify the installation by running:

```css
Copy code
ng --version
```

1. This will display the installed version of Angular CLI, confirming that it's ready to use.

Creating Your First Angular Application

Now that Angular CLI is installed, let's create a new Angular project.

1. **Generate a New Project**: Open a terminal or command prompt and navigate to the directory where you want to create the project. Run the following command:

```arduino
Copy code
ng new MyFirstAngularApp
```

1. This will prompt you to choose some options:

- **Would you like to add Angular routing?**: Select **Yes**.
- **Which stylesheet format would you like to use?**: Select **CSS** (or choose another format like SCSS or SASS if you prefer).

1. **Navigate to the Project Directory**: After the project is created, navigate to the project folder:

CHAPTER 1: GETTING STARTED WITH ASP.NET CORE AND ANGULAR

```bash
Copy code
cd MyFirstAngularApp
```

1. **Serve the Application**: To run the application, use the ng serve command:

```
Copy code
ng serve
```

1. This will start the development server, and you can view your Angular application by opening a browser and navigating to http://localhost:4200. You should see the default Angular welcome page, confirming that the application is running.

Congratulations! You've successfully created your first Angular application using Angular CLI. In the next chapters, we'll explore how to integrate this Angular front-end with the ASP.NET Core MVC back-end to build a full-stack web application.

Chapter 2: Understanding MVC Architecture in ASP.NET Core

Web applications have evolved over the years, moving from simple, static pages to more complex, dynamic systems. The introduction of various design patterns, like the Model-View-Controller (MVC) pattern, has provided developers with a structured way to build scalable and maintainable applications. ASP.NET Core embraces this design pattern, allowing developers to separate their application's concerns logically.

This chapter will give you a detailed understanding of the MVC architecture in ASP.NET Core, explaining its components (Model, View, Controller) and how they interact. We will also walk through building a simple MVC application to solidify your understanding.

What is MVC (Model-View-Controller)?

Model-View-Controller (MVC) is a design pattern used to separate the concerns of an application into three interconnected components:

1. **Model**: Represents the data and business logic of the application. The model interacts with the database, manages data, and enforces business rules.

2. **View**: Represents the presentation layer. It handles how data is displayed to the user, usually through HTML pages. The view is responsible for rendering the user interface based on the data provided by the model.
3. **Controller**: Acts as an intermediary between the model and the view. It processes user input, interacts with the model to retrieve or manipulate data, and then determines which view to render in response.

The primary goal of the MVC pattern is to separate concerns:

- The **Model** focuses on the data and business logic.
- The **View** focuses on the presentation and user interface.
- The **Controller** focuses on the flow of data and user interactions.

This separation makes the application easier to manage, maintain, and scale because each component can be developed and tested independently.

Benefits of MVC Architecture

1. **Separation of Concerns**: By dividing the application into three distinct components, developers can focus on specific aspects of the application without affecting others. For example, a designer can modify the UI (View) without changing the business logic (Model).
2. **Scalability**: MVC allows applications to grow and scale easily. As the application grows, the separation of concerns helps manage the complexity more effectively.
3. **Maintainability**: Since the MVC pattern promotes modular code, applications become easier to maintain. Bugs can be fixed and features added without introducing unintended side effects in other parts of the application.
4. **Testability**: MVC makes it easier to test applications. Each component (Model, View, and Controller) can be tested independently, which leads to better unit testing and less complex debugging.

In ASP.NET Core, the MVC pattern is deeply integrated, providing a robust foundation for building web applications. Let's now see how MVC works in the ASP.NET Core framework.

How MVC Works in ASP.NET Core

In ASP.NET Core, the MVC pattern works by mapping incoming HTTP requests to controller actions, interacting with the model, and rendering the appropriate view in response. ASP.NET Core MVC provides a framework for building web applications and APIs using the MVC design pattern.

The process of how ASP.NET Core MVC handles a request can be summarized in the following steps:

1. **Request Routing**: When a user makes a request to an ASP.NET Core application, the request is processed through the **routing middleware**. Routing determines which controller and action method will handle the request based on the URL.
2. **Controller Action Execution**: Once the appropriate controller and action method are determined by routing, the controller interacts with the model to retrieve data or perform operations. The controller processes the input, invokes business logic, and determines which view to render (if applicable).
3. **View Rendering**: The controller passes the data (usually as a model) to the view, which renders the HTML markup based on the model's data and returns it as the HTTP response to the user.

This flow ensures that the responsibilities are clearly defined and distributed across the three components: Controllers handle the requests and manage the application's flow, Models handle the business logic and data, and Views manage the presentation layer.

Routing in ASP.NET Core MVC

Routing is a critical part of ASP.NET Core MVC. When a user sends a request to the application, routing is responsible for mapping the URL to a specific controller and action method. The default route configuration in

CHAPTER 2: UNDERSTANDING MVC ARCHITECTURE IN ASP.NET CORE

ASP.NET Core MVC is defined in the Startup.cs file, where the Configure method sets up the routing system.

For example, consider the following default routing configuration:

```csharp
Copy code
app.UseEndpoints(endpoints =>
{
    endpoints.MapControllerRoute(
        name: "default",
        pattern: "{controller=Home}/{action=Index}/{id?}");
});
```

This routing pattern translates URLs into controller action calls. For instance:

- **/Home/Index**: The request is mapped to the Index action method of the HomeController.
- **/Products/Details/5**: This URL would route the request to the Details action method of the ProductsController, passing an id parameter with the value 5.

The default route consists of:

- **Controller**: The first part of the URL represents the controller (e.g., Home, Products).
- **Action**: The second part of the URL represents the action method in the controller (e.g., Index, Details).
- **Parameters**: Optional parameters (e.g., id) can be passed to the action method.

Next, let's break down the core components of the MVC pattern in ASP.NET Core: Controllers, Models, and Views.

Controllers: Handling HTTP Requests

Controllers in ASP.NET Core are classes that handle incoming HTTP requests. A controller is responsible for handling user input, processing data through the model, and determining which view to render as a response.

Controllers are located in the **Controllers** folder of an ASP.NET Core project. Each controller is a class that inherits from the Controller base class and is responsible for defining action methods. Action methods respond to user requests and perform the necessary operations, such as querying the database or updating data.

Creating a Controller

To create a controller in ASP.NET Core MVC, follow these steps:

1. **Create a New Controller Class**: In the **Controllers** folder, create a new class. By convention, controller classes have the suffix "Controller". For example, create a HomeController:

```csharp
Copy code
public class HomeController : Controller
{
    public IActionResult Index()
    {
        return View();
    }
}
```

1. In this example:

- The HomeController class inherits from the Controller base class.
- The Index action method returns a view to be rendered.

1. **Action Methods**: Each action method in the controller corresponds

to a specific HTTP request. Action methods typically return an IActionResult, which can represent different types of responses, such as a view, a redirect, or a JSON result.

2. Here's an example of multiple action methods in a controller:

```csharp
Copy code
public class ProductsController : Controller
{
    public IActionResult List()
    {
        // Logic to retrieve product list
        return View();
    }

    public IActionResult Details(int id)
    {
        // Logic to retrieve product details by id
        return View();
    }
}
```

1. In this example:

- The List method handles requests for listing products.
- The Details method accepts a product ID as a parameter and returns the details of the product.

Returning Results from Controllers

ASP.NET Core MVC provides various return types for controller action methods. The most commonly used are:

- **View()**: Returns a view to the client (typically an HTML page).
- **RedirectToAction()**: Redirects the user to another action method.

- **Json()**: Returns data in JSON format, which is especially useful for APIs.
- **Content()**: Returns plain text or other content types.

For example, here's how to return different types of responses:

```csharp
Copy code
public class ExampleController : Controller
{
    public IActionResult Index()
    {
        return View(); // Returns a view
    }

    public IActionResult RedirectToHome()
    {
        return RedirectToAction("Index", "Home"); // Redirects to Home/Index
    }

    public IActionResult GetJsonData()
    {
        var data = new { Name = "John", Age = 30 };
        return Json(data); // Returns JSON data
    }

    public IActionResult GetPlainText()
    {
        return Content("Hello, World!"); // Returns plain text
    }
}
```

Controllers act as the backbone of the MVC framework, processing requests, interacting with the model, and returning the appropriate response. Let's now explore how models handle data and business logic in ASP.NET Core.

Models: Defining Your Data

The **Model** in MVC represents the application's data and business logic. Models are responsible for interacting with the database, validating data, and defining rules for the data. In ASP.NET Core, models can be plain C# classes (also known as POCOs, or Plain Old CLR Objects) that represent entities in the application.

Creating a Model

In ASP.NET Core, models are usually placed in the **Models** folder. Models can be created as simple classes that define the properties representing the data.

Here's an example of a simple Product model:

```csharp
Copy code
public class Product
{
    public int Id { get; set; }
    public string Name { get; set; }
    public decimal Price { get; set; }
    public string Description { get; set; }
}
```

This Product model defines the structure of a product entity with properties such as Id, Name, Price, and Description.

Interacting with Databases

To interact with a database, you typically use **Entity Framework Core** (EF Core), which is an Object-Relational Mapping (ORM) framework for .NET. EF Core allows you to work with databases using C# objects instead of writing raw SQL queries.

To use EF Core, you need to install the necessary NuGet packages. Open your project in Visual Studio, right-click on the project in the Solution Explorer, and select **Manage NuGet Packages**. Search for and install the following packages:

- Microsoft.EntityFrameworkCore
- Microsoft.EntityFrameworkCore.SqlServer (or another database provider)
- Microsoft.EntityFrameworkCore.Tools

After installing the packages, you can create a **DbContext** class, which represents a session with the database and allows you to query and save data. Here's an example of a StoreDbContext class:

```csharp
Copy code
public class StoreDbContext : DbContext
{
    public StoreDbContext (DbContextOptions<StoreDbContext> options)
    : base(options)
    {
    }

    public DbSet<Product> Products { get; set; }
}
```

In this example, StoreDbContext inherits from DbContext, and the Products property represents the table for the Product model in the database.

Setting Up Database Configuration

To configure the database connection string, you need to update the appsettings.json file in your project. Add a connection string to your database:

```json
Copy code
{
  "ConnectionStrings": {
    "DefaultConnection":
    "Server=your_server;Database=YourDatabaseName;Trusted_Connection=True;
```

CHAPTER 2: UNDERSTANDING MVC ARCHITECTURE IN ASP.NET CORE

```
MultipleActiveResultSets=true"
    },
    // other settings
}
```

In your Startup.cs file, you need to configure the DbContext to use the connection string:

```csharp
Copy code
public void ConfigureServices
(IServiceCollection services)
{
    services.AddDbContext<StoreDbContext>(options =>
        options.UseSqlServer(Configuration.
GetConnectionString
("DefaultConnection")));

    services.AddControllersWithViews();
}
```

This setup ensures that your application can connect to the specified database and perform CRUD operations using the Product model.

Views: Rendering the UI

The **View** in MVC is responsible for rendering the user interface and presenting data to the user. Views in ASP.NET Core are typically Razor views, which use the Razor syntax to combine HTML markup with C# code.

Razor views are stored in the **Views** folder, typically organized into subfolders based on the controller. For example, views related to the ProductsController would be stored in Views/Products.

Creating a Razor View

To create a Razor view, follow these steps:

1. **Add a New View**: Right-click on the appropriate controller folder (e.g., Views/Products) and select **Add** > **New Item**. Choose **Razor View** and name it (e.g., Index.cshtml).
2. **Write Razor Syntax**: Open the newly created Razor view and write the HTML markup along with Razor syntax to display data. Here's an example of a simple view that displays a list of products:

```razor
Copy code
@model IEnumerable<Product>

<h1>Product List</h1>

<table class="table">
    <thead>
        <tr>
            <th>Id</th>
            <th>Name</th>
            <th>Price</th>
            <th>Description</th>
        </tr>
    </thead>
    <tbody>
        @foreach (var product in Model)
        {
            <tr>
                <td>@product.Id</td>
                <td>@product.Name</td>
                <td>@product.Price.ToString("C")</td>
                <td>@product.Description</td>
            </tr>
        }
    </tbody>
</table>
```

In this example:

- The @model directive at the top indicates that the view expects a collection of Product objects.
- The Razor syntax is used to loop through the model and render each product in an HTML table.

Returning Views from Controllers

To render the Index view from the ProductsController, you would modify the action method like this:

```csharp
Copy code
public class ProductsController : Controller
{
    private readonly StoreDbContext _context;

    public ProductsController(StoreDbContext context)
    {
        _context = context;
    }

    public IActionResult Index()
    {
        var products = _context.Products.ToList();
        return View(products); // Passing the list of products to the view
    }
}
```

In this example, the Index action method retrieves the list of products from the database using the DbContext and passes it to the view for rendering.

Building a Simple MVC Application

Now that you have an understanding of the MVC architecture and its components in ASP.NET Core, let's build a simple MVC application to bring it all together. This application will allow users to manage a list of products by performing basic CRUD operations: Create, Read, Update, and Delete.

Step-by-Step Guide to Building a Simple MVC Application

1. **Create a New ASP.NET Core MVC Project**: Use Visual Studio to create a new ASP.NET Core Web Application. Select the MVC template when prompted.
2. **Add the Product Model**: Create a Product model in the **Models** folder:

```csharp
Copy code
public class Product
{
    public int Id { get; set; }
    public string Name { get; set; }
    public decimal Price { get; set; }
    public string Description { get; set; }
}
```

1. **Set Up the Database Context**: Create a new class StoreDbContext in the **Models** folder and configure it to include the Products DbSet.
2. **Configure Connection String**: Update appsettings.json with your database connection string, and configure the DbContext in Startup.cs.
3. **Add Products Controller**: Create a ProductsController in the **Controllers** folder. Implement the following action methods:

```csharp
Copy code
public class ProductsController : Controller
{
    private readonly StoreDbContext _context;

    public ProductsController(StoreDbContext context)
    {
        _context = context;
```

CHAPTER 2: UNDERSTANDING MVC ARCHITECTURE IN ASP.NET CORE

```csharp
    }

    // GET: Products
    public IActionResult Index()
    {
        var products = _context.Products.ToList();
        return View(products);
    }

    // GET: Products/Create
    public IActionResult Create()
    {
        return View();
    }

    // POST: Products/Create
    [HttpPost]
    [ValidateAntiForgeryToken]
    public IActionResult Create(Product product)
    {
        if (ModelState.IsValid)
        {
            _context.Products.Add(product);
            _context.SaveChanges();
            return RedirectToAction(nameof(Index));
        }
        return View(product);
    }
}
```

1. **Create Razor Views**: In the **Views/Products** folder, create the following Razor views:

- Index.cshtml for listing products.
- Create.cshtml for adding a new product.

1. **Implement Create View**:

```razor
@model Product

<h1>Create Product</h1>

<form asp-action="Create">
    <div class="form-group">
        <label asp-for="Name"></label>
        <input asp-for="Name" class="form-control" />
        <span asp-validation-for="Name" class="text-danger"></span>
    </div>
    <div class="form-group">
        <label asp-for="Price"></label>
        <input asp-for="Price" class="form-control" />
        <span asp-validation-for="Price" class="text-danger"></span>
    </div>
    <div class="form-group">
        <label asp-for="Description"></label>
        <textarea asp-for="Description" class="form-control"></textarea>
        <span asp-validation-for="Description" class="text-danger"></span>
    </div>
    <button type="submit" class="btn btn-primary">Create</button>
</form>
```

1. **Run Migrations**: Use the Package Manager Console to run migrations and create the database:

```sql
Copy code
Add-Migration InitialCreate
Update-Database
```

1. **Run the Application**: Press **F5** to run the application. You should be able to navigate to /Products to view the list of products and /Products/Create to add new products.

Conclusion

In this chapter, we explored the Model-View-Controller (MVC) architecture and how it is implemented in ASP.NET Core. We discussed the roles of Controllers, Models, and Views, and we walked through the steps to build a simple MVC application that manages a list of products.

Chapter 3: Angular Fundamentals

Introduction

Angular is one of the most popular front-end frameworks used in web development today. Its ability to create highly dynamic, responsive, and scalable single-page applications (SPAs) makes it a preferred choice for many developers and enterprises. In this chapter, we will dive into the core concepts of Angular and explore how its modules, components, and directives work together to build efficient web applications. You will also learn the basics of TypeScript, Angular's primary programming language, how data binding functions within Angular, the component lifecycle, and how to create and manage components.

Core Concepts of Angular (Modules, Components, and Directives)

Modules

In Angular, modules play a critical role in organizing the application structure. A module is a container that holds related pieces of an application, such as components, services, directives, and pipes. Every Angular application has at least one module, known as the **root module**, which is typically named AppModule.

Modules are used to group functionality, making it easier to manage and maintain the codebase. As your application grows in size and complexity, dividing it into multiple modules helps organize it logically, ensuring a modular structure that promotes scalability.

- **NgModule Decorator**: Modules are defined using the @NgModule decorator in Angular. This decorator takes an object with metadata properties that define the module's components, directives, pipes, and services. Here's a typical example of a module:

```typescript
Copy code
import { NgModule } from '@angular/core';
import { BrowserModule } from '@angular/platform-browser';
import { AppComponent } from './app.component';

@NgModule({
  declarations: [
    AppComponent
  ],
  imports: [
    BrowserModule
  ],
  providers: [],
  bootstrap: [AppComponent]
})
export class AppModule { }
```

In this example, the AppModule contains the root component (AppComponent) and imports the BrowserModule, which is necessary for any Angular application running in the browser.

Components

Components are the building blocks of an Angular application. A component is a class that interacts with the view and handles the business logic for a specific part of the UI. Every Angular application consists of multiple components, each responsible for rendering a piece of the user interface.

A component is defined using the @Component decorator, which provides metadata such as the selector, template, and styles that define how the component should behave and be displayed.

Example of a simple Angular component:

```typescript
Copy code
import { Component } from '@angular/core';

@Component({
  selector: 'app-hello-world',
  template: `<h1>Hello, World!</h1>`,
  styles: [`
    h1 {
      color: blue;
    }
  `]
})
export class HelloWorldComponent { }
```

In this example:

- The @Component decorator defines the metadata for the component.
- The selector is the custom HTML element (<app-hello-world>) used to insert the component into the DOM.
- The template is the HTML markup rendered by the component.
- The styles define the component's CSS styling.

The relationship between components forms the structure of an Angular application. Each component is typically part of a **tree** of components, where the root component (often called AppComponent) serves as the entry point, and other components are nested within it.

Directives

Directives in Angular are special markers or attributes in the DOM that tell Angular to do something to that DOM element or its children. They come in three types:

1. **Component Directives**: These are the most common type of directive

in Angular. Every Angular component is a directive with a template.
2. **Structural Directives**: These alter the structure of the DOM by adding, removing, or manipulating elements. Examples include *ngIf (which conditionally adds or removes elements) and *ngFor (which repeats a section of the DOM for each item in a list).
3. **Attribute Directives**: These modify the behavior or appearance of an element. A common example is ngClass, which dynamically sets CSS classes.

Example of a structural directive (*ngIf):

```html
Copy code
<p *ngIf="isVisible">This paragraph is visible if 'isVisible' is true.</p>
```

Here, the paragraph will only be displayed if the isVisible property is true.

Directives are a powerful tool in Angular that enhance the HTML capabilities, allowing developers to create dynamic and responsive UIs. Now that we've covered the core concepts of modules, components, and directives, let's move on to the basics of TypeScript, the language that powers Angular.

TypeScript Basics for Angular

Angular is written in **TypeScript**, a superset of JavaScript that introduces static typing and modern JavaScript features. TypeScript provides several advantages over traditional JavaScript, including:

- **Type Safety**: With static types, developers can catch errors at compile time rather than at runtime.
- **Improved Tooling**: TypeScript offers better autocompletion, refactoring, and navigation features in most IDEs.
- **ES6+ Features**: TypeScript supports features like classes, interfaces, arrow functions, and async/await, which makes writing and managing

code easier and more readable.

Type Annotations

One of the fundamental features of TypeScript is **type annotations**, which allow you to explicitly declare the data types of variables, parameters, and function return types. This leads to better error detection and improved code clarity.

Here's a basic example of type annotations:

```typescript
Copy code
let username: string = 'JohnDoe';
let age: number = 30;
let isLoggedIn: boolean = true;

function greet(user: string): string {
  return `Hello, ${user}`;
}
```

In this example:

- username is explicitly declared as a string.
- age is a number.
- isLoggedIn is a boolean.
- The greet function takes a string as a parameter and returns a string.

Interfaces

TypeScript introduces **interfaces**, which allow you to define the shape of an object. Interfaces are useful for ensuring that objects have the expected structure.

Here's an example of an interface:

```typescript
Copy code
```

```
interface User {
  id: number;
  name: string;
  email: string;
}

let user: User = {
  id: 1,
  name: 'John Doe',
  email: 'john@example.com'
};
```

In this example, the User interface defines the expected structure of a user object, which includes an id, name, and email. TypeScript will ensure that any object assigned to the user variable follows this structure.

Classes

In TypeScript (and Angular), **classes** are used to define blueprints for creating objects. Classes in TypeScript support inheritance, encapsulation, and polymorphism, making it easy to organize code into reusable units.

Here's an example of a simple class:

```typescript
Copy code
class Person {
  name: string;
  age: number;

  constructor(name: string, age: number) {
    this.name = name;
    this.age = age;
  }

  greet() {
    return `Hello, my name is ${this.name} and I am ${this.age} years old.`;
  }
}
```

```
let person = new Person('Jane', 25);
console.log(person.greet());
```

In this example:

- The Person class has two properties: name and age.
- The constructor method initializes the class with values.
- The greet method returns a string introducing the person.

By using TypeScript in Angular, developers can write cleaner, more reliable code that scales well as the application grows. Now, let's explore **data binding**, one of the core features that make Angular powerful and user-friendly.

Data Binding in Angular (Interpolation, Property Binding, Event Binding)

Data binding in Angular refers to the process of synchronizing data between the component (TypeScript code) and the view (HTML). Angular provides different forms of data binding that enable the flow of information between the model (component class) and the view (template).

1. Interpolation

Interpolation is used to display dynamic data from the component in the view. It's done by placing expressions inside double curly braces {{ }} within the template.

Example of interpolation:

```typescript
Copy code
@Component({
  selector: 'app-profile',
  template: `<h1>Welcome, {{ username }}</h1>`
})
```

```
export class ProfileComponent {
  username: string = 'John Doe';
}
```

In this example, the username property is interpolated into the template and displayed as part of the heading.

Interpolation is one-way data binding, meaning that data flows from the component to the view but not the other way around.

2. Property Binding

Property binding is used to bind the properties of HTML elements to values in the component. It's a form of one-way data binding, where data flows from the component to the view.

Syntax of property binding:

```html
Copy code
<img [src]="imageUrl">
```

Here's an example:

```typescript
Copy code
@Component({
  selector: 'app-user',
  template: `<img [src]="profilePictureUrl" alt="Profile Picture">`
})
export class UserComponent {
  profilePictureUrl: string = 'https://example.com/profile.jpg';
}
```

In this example, the src attribute of the img element is bound to the profilePictureUrl property in the component, and the image will be displayed based on the URL provided.

3. Event Binding

Event binding is used to listen for and respond to user interactions, such as clicks, input changes, or form submissions. It allows the component to react to events that occur in the view.

Syntax for event binding:

```html
Copy code
<button (click)="onClick()">Click Me</button>
```

Example of event binding:

```typescript
Copy code
@Component({
  selector: 'app-button',
  template: `<button (click)="greet()">Greet</button>`
})
export class ButtonComponent {
  greet() {
    alert('Hello!');
  }
}
```

In this example, when the button is clicked, the greet method is called, and a greeting alert is displayed.

4. Two-Way Data Binding

Two-way data binding allows data to flow in both directions, from the component to the view and from the view to the component. This is especially useful for forms, where user input needs to be captured and stored in the component.

In Angular, two-way data binding is achieved using the [(ngModel)] directive:

```html
Copy code
```

```
<input [(ngModel)]="username" placeholder="Enter your name">
<p>Your name is {{ username }}</p>
```

In this example, the username property is bound to the input field, allowing the user to type their name, which is immediately reflected in the paragraph below.

For two-way data binding to work, you must import the FormsModule in your module:

```
typescript
Copy code
import { FormsModule } from '@angular/forms';

@NgModule({
  imports: [FormsModule],
  // other imports and declarations
})
export class AppModule { }
```

Data binding in Angular simplifies the process of creating dynamic and interactive user interfaces by seamlessly connecting the data and view. Next, let's explore the **component lifecycle**, which helps you manage the state of components during their existence.

Component Lifecycle

Angular components go through a lifecycle from the moment they are instantiated until they are destroyed. Understanding the component lifecycle is crucial for managing component initialization, data fetching, cleanup tasks, and reacting to changes in component properties.

Angular provides a series of lifecycle hooks that allow developers to execute code at specific points during a component's life. These hooks are methods that can be implemented in a component class to respond to lifecycle events.

1. ngOnInit

ngOnInit is one of the most commonly used lifecycle hooks. It is called once, after Angular has initialized the component's input properties and rendered the view.

```typescript
Copy code
@Component({
  selector: 'app-lifecycle',
  template: `<p>Component Initialized</p>`
})
export class LifecycleComponent implements OnInit {
  ngOnInit() {
    console.log('ngOnInit: Component has been initialized.');
  }
}
```

In this example, the ngOnInit method will be called after the component is initialized, and the message will be logged to the console.

2. ngOnChanges

ngOnChanges is called when the input properties of a component change. It's particularly useful when the component relies on external data passed down from a parent component.

```typescript
Copy code
@Component({
  selector: 'app-child',
  template: `<p>{{ data }}</p>`
})
export class ChildComponent implements OnChanges {
  @Input() data: string;

  ngOnChanges(changes: SimpleChanges) {
    console.log('ngOnChanges: Data changed:',
    changes.data.currentValue);
  }
}
```

In this example, whenever the data property changes, the ngOnChanges hook is triggered, and the new value is logged.

3. ngDoCheck

ngDoCheck is called during every change detection cycle, allowing you to implement custom change detection logic.

```typescript
Copy code
@Component({
  selector: 'app-check',
  template: `<p>{{ counter }}</p>`
})
export class CheckComponent implements DoCheck {
  counter: number = 0;

  ngDoCheck() {
    this.counter++;
    console.log('ngDoCheck: Change detection cycle:',
    this.counter);
  }
}
```

4. ngAfterViewInit and ngAfterViewChecked

ngAfterViewInit is called after Angular has fully initialized the component's view and its child views. It is often used to perform tasks that require the view to be fully rendered, such as DOM manipulation.

ngAfterViewChecked is called after every change detection cycle, allowing you to react to any changes in the view.

```typescript
Copy code
@Component({
  selector: 'app-view',
  template: `<p>View Content</p>`
})
export class ViewComponent implements AfterViewInit,
AfterViewChecked {
  ngAfterViewInit() {
```

```
    console.log('ngAfterViewInit: View initialized.');
  }

  ngAfterViewChecked() {
    console.log('ngAfterViewChecked: View checked.');
  }
}
```

5. ngOnDestroy

ngOnDestroy is called just before the component is destroyed. It's typically used to clean up resources, such as unsubscribing from observables or detaching event listeners.

```typescript
Copy code
@Component({
  selector: 'app-destroy',
  template: `<p>Destroying Component</p>`
})
export class DestroyComponent implements OnDestroy {
  ngOnDestroy() {
    console.log('ngOnDestroy: Component is about to be
    destroyed.');
  }
}
```

The component lifecycle in Angular gives you control over the initialization, updating, and destruction of your components, ensuring that your application runs efficiently.

Creating and Managing Angular Components

Now that you have a solid understanding of Angular's core concepts, data binding, and lifecycle hooks, it's time to learn how to create and manage components effectively.

1. Creating a Component Using Angular CLI

Angular CLI makes it easy to create components using the ng generate command. The command automatically generates the necessary files for a component, including the TypeScript class, template, style, and test files.

To create a new component, run the following command:

```bash
Copy code
ng generate component my-new-component
```

This command will create the following files in the src/app directory:

- my-new-component.component.ts: The TypeScript class for the component.
- my-new-component.component.html: The template file for the component's view.
- my-new-component.component.css: The stylesheet for the component.
- my-new-component.component.spec.ts: The test file for the component.

After generating the component, it is automatically declared in the AppModule and can be used in other components by adding the <app-my-new-component> tag to the HTML template.

2. Nesting Components

Components in Angular can be nested, meaning that one component can contain other components. This allows for a modular structure where complex UIs are built from smaller, reusable components.

For example, you can create a ProductListComponent that contains multiple ProductItemComponent instances:

```html
Copy code
<!-- product-list.component.html -->
<app-product-item *ngFor="let product of products"
[product]="product"></app-product-item>
```

Here, the ProductListComponent iterates over a list of products and passes each product to a ProductItemComponent.

3. Passing Data Between Components

In Angular, data can be passed between parent and child components using **input** and **output** properties.

- **@Input()**: Used to pass data from the parent component to the child component.
- **@Output()**: Used to emit events from the child component to the parent component.

Example of using @Input() to pass data to a child component:

```typescript
Copy code
// child.component.ts
@Component({
  selector: 'app-child',
  template: `<p>{{ message }}</p>`
})
export class ChildComponent {
  @Input() message: string;
}
```

```html
Copy code
<!-- parent.component.html -->
<app-child [message]="parentMessage"></app-child>
```

In this example, the parentMessage from the parent component is passed to the message property in the child component.

4. Reusing Components

One of the key benefits of components is reusability. Once a component is created, it can be used multiple times across the application, reducing redundancy and simplifying maintenance.

For instance, a ButtonComponent could be reused across various pages in an application:

```html
html
Copy code
<app-button [label]="'Submit'"></app-button>
<app-button [label]="'Cancel'"></app-button>
```

5. Managing Component Styles

Angular components can have their own styles defined using the styles or styleUrls property in the @Component decorator. These styles are encapsulated within the component, ensuring that they do not affect other components.

```typescript
typescript
Copy code
@Component({
  selector: 'app-styled',
  template: `<p>Styled component</p>`,
  styles: [`
    p {
      color: red;
    }
  `]
})
export class StyledComponent { }
```

In this example, the paragraph will be styled with red text, but this style will not affect other components in the application.

Conclusion

In this chapter, we explored the **core fundamentals of Angular**, focusing on modules, components, directives, TypeScript basics, data binding, and the component lifecycle. We also covered how to create and manage components, the building blocks of Angular applications.

Chapter 4: Building Your First Full-Stack Application

Introduction

In this chapter, we will embark on an exciting journey to build a full-stack application using ASP.NET Core for the backend and Angular for the frontend. By the end of this chapter, you will have a working application that demonstrates how to connect the two frameworks, create RESTful APIs, and deploy your application locally.

We will start by discussing the project structure suitable for full-stack development, then move on to setting up the backend using ASP.NET Core, creating RESTful APIs, connecting the Angular frontend to the ASP.NET Core backend, and finally deploying the application locally.

Project Structure for Full-Stack Development

A well-organized project structure is essential for maintaining clarity and ease of development in a full-stack application. When combining ASP.NET Core with Angular, we can separate the frontend and backend into distinct projects within the same solution. This separation allows for cleaner code management and makes it easier to develop and deploy each part independently.

Recommended Project Structure

Here's a recommended structure for organizing a full-stack application with ASP.NET Core and Angular:

```scss
Copy code
MyFullStackApp |  ├───
    backend              // ASP.NET Core project |  ├───
        Controllers      // API Controllers |  ├───
        Models           // Data Models |  ├───
        Data             // Data Access Layer |  ├───
        Services         // Business Logic Layer |  ├───
        Migrations       // Entity Framework
        Migrations |  ├───
        appsettings.json // Configuration settings |  └───
        Startup.cs       // Application Startup
        Configuration |  └───

    frontend             // Angular project ├───
        src |  ├───
            app          // Angular components and
            modules |  ├───
            assets       // Images, styles, etc. |  ├───
            environments // Environment configuration |  └───
            index.html   // Main HTML file ├───
        angular.json     // Angular CLI configuration ├───
        package.json     // NPM dependencies and scripts └───
        tsconfig.json    // TypeScript configuration
```

1. *Setting Up a Backend in ASP.NET Core*

To begin building our full-stack application, we need to set up the backend using ASP.NET Core. This backend will be responsible for handling requests, managing data, and exposing RESTful APIs that the Angular frontend will consume.

Step 1: Create a New ASP.NET Core Web API Project

1. **Open Visual Studio**: Launch Visual Studio and select **Create a new project**.
2. **Select the Template**: Choose **ASP.NET Core Web API** from the list of templates. Click **Next**.
3. **Configure the Project**: Name your project (e.g., MyFullStackApp.Backend), choose a location, and click **Create**.
4. **Set Up the Project**: In the next dialog, choose **.NET 6.0 (or later)** as the framework. Ensure that **Enable OpenAPI Support** is checked for API documentation. Click **Create**.

Now you have a new ASP.NET Core Web API project set up.

Step 2: Configure the Data Models

In our backend, we will need a data model to represent the entities in our application. For this example, we will create a simple Product model.

1. **Create a Models Folder**: Right-click on the project in the Solution Explorer, select **Add > New Folder**, and name it **Models**.
2. **Create the Product Model**: Right-click the **Models** folder, select **Add > Class**, and name it Product.cs. Add the following properties to the class:

```csharp
Copy code
namespace MyFullStackApp.Backend.Models
{
    public class Product
    {
        public int Id { get; set; }
        public string Name { get; set; }
        public decimal Price { get; set; }
        public string Description { get; set; }
```

CHAPTER 4: BUILDING YOUR FIRST FULL-STACK APPLICATION

```
    }
}
```

Step 3: Set Up Entity Framework Core

To interact with a database, we will use **Entity Framework Core**. This ORM simplifies data access by allowing us to work with C# objects instead of writing raw SQL.

1. **Install Entity Framework Core Packages**: Open the **Package Manager Console** in Visual Studio (Tools > NuGet Package Manager > Package Manager Console) and run the following commands:

```powershell
Copy code
Install-Package Microsoft.EntityFrameworkCore.SqlServer
Install-Package Microsoft.EntityFrameworkCore.Tools
```

1. **Create the DbContext**: In the **Models** folder, create a new class called ApplicationDbContext.cs and configure it as follows:

```csharp
Copy code
using Microsoft.EntityFrameworkCore;

namespace MyFullStackApp.Backend.Models
{
    public class ApplicationDbContext : DbContext
    {
        public ApplicationDbContext(DbContextOptions<ApplicationDbContext> options)
            : base(options)
        {
        }
```

```
    public DbSet<Product> Products { get; set; }
  }
}
```

1. **Configure the Connection String**: Open appsettings.json and add a connection string for your database:

```json
Copy code
{
  "ConnectionStrings": {
    "DefaultConnection": "Server=your_server;Database=YourDatabase;Trusted_Connection=True;MultipleActiveResultSets=true"
  },
  // Other settings...
}
```

1. **Configure Services in Startup.cs**: Open Startup.cs and add the following code in the ConfigureServices method to register the ApplicationDbContext:

```csharp
Copy code
public void ConfigureServices(IServiceCollection services)
{
    services.AddDbContext<ApplicationDbContext>(options =>
        options.UseSqlServer(Configuration.GetConnectionString("DefaultConnection")));
```

CHAPTER 4: BUILDING YOUR FIRST FULL-STACK APPLICATION

```
    services.AddControllers();
    services.AddEndpointsApiExplorer();
    services.AddSwaggerGen();
}
```

Step 4: Create RESTful APIs in ASP.NET Core

With our models and database context set up, we can now create RESTful APIs for our products.

1. **Create a Controllers Folder**: Right-click on the project, select **Add > New Folder**, and name it **Controllers**.
2. **Create the ProductsController**: Right-click on the **Controllers** folder, select **Add > Controller**, and choose **API Controller - Empty**. Name it ProductsController.cs.
3. **Implement CRUD Operations**: Open ProductsController.cs and implement the following code:

```csharp
Copy code
using Microsoft.AspNetCore.Mvc;
using Microsoft.EntityFrameworkCore;
using MyFullStackApp.Backend.Models;

namespace MyFullStackApp.Backend.Controllers
{
    [Route("api/[controller]")]
    [ApiController]
    public class ProductsController : ControllerBase
    {
        private readonly ApplicationDbContext _context;

        public ProductsController
(ApplicationDbContext context)
```

```csharp
        {
            _context = context;
        }

        // GET: api/products
        [HttpGet]
        public async Task<ActionResult
<IEnumerable<Product>>> GetProducts()
        {
            return await _context.Products.ToListAsync();
        }

        // GET: api/products/5
        [HttpGet("{id}")]
        public async Task<ActionResult
<Product>> GetProduct(int id)
        {
            var product = await _context.Products.FindAsync(id);

            if (product == null)
            {
                return NotFound();
            }

            return product;
        }

        // POST: api/products
        [HttpPost]
        public async Task<ActionResult<
Product>> PostProduct(Product product)
        {
            _context.Products.Add(product);
            await _context.SaveChangesAsync();

            return CreatedAtAction(nameof(GetProduct), new
{ id = product.Id }, product);
        }
```

CHAPTER 4: BUILDING YOUR FIRST FULL-STACK APPLICATION

```csharp
// PUT: api/products/5
[HttpPut("{id}")]
public async Task<IActionResult> PutProduct(int id,
Product product)
{
    if (id != product.Id)
    {
        return BadRequest();
    }

    _context.Entry(product).State = EntityState.Modified;

    try
    {
        await _context.SaveChangesAsync();
    }
    catch (DbUpdateConcurrencyException)
    {
        if (!ProductExists(id))
        {
            return NotFound();
        }
        else
        {
            throw;
        }
    }

    return NoContent();
}

// DELETE: api/products/5
[HttpDelete("{id}")]
public async Task<IActionResult> DeleteProduct(int id)
{
    var product = await _context.Products.FindAsync(id);
    if (product == null)
    {
```

```
                return NotFound();
            }

            _context.Products.Remove(product);
            await _context.SaveChangesAsync();

            return NoContent();
        }

        private bool ProductExists(int id)
        {
            return _context.Products.Any(e => e.Id == id);
        }
    }
}
```

In this controller:

- The GetProducts method retrieves all products.
- The GetProduct method retrieves a product by its ID.
- The PostProduct method adds a new product.
- The PutProduct method updates an existing product.
- The DeleteProduct method removes a product.

Step 5: Enable Swagger for API Documentation

To make testing your API easier, you can use Swagger, a tool for generating API documentation.

1. **Add Swagger to Your Project**: Make sure you have the Swagger packages installed. If not, add them using the following command in the Package Manager Console:

```powershell
Copy code
```

CHAPTER 4: BUILDING YOUR FIRST FULL-STACK APPLICATION

```
Install-Package Swashbuckle.AspNetCore
```

1. **Configure Swagger in Startup.cs**: In the ConfigureServices method, add the following line to enable Swagger:

```csharp
Copy code
services.AddSwaggerGen();
```

1. **Configure Swagger in the HTTP Request Pipeline**: In the Configure method, add the following code to enable Swagger UI:

```csharp
Copy code
app.UseSwagger();
app.UseSwaggerUI(c =>
{
    c.SwaggerEndpoint("/swagger/v1/swagger.json", "My API V1");
});
```

1. **Run the Application**: Press **F5** to run the application. Navigate to http://localhost:5000/swagger in your browser to access the Swagger UI, where you can test your API endpoints.

Connecting Angular Frontend to ASP.NET Core Backend

With the backend API ready, it's time to connect the Angular frontend to the ASP.NET Core backend. This will allow the Angular application to consume the RESTful APIs we created.

Step 1: Create an Angular Project

If you haven't already, create a new Angular project in a separate folder from your backend.

1. **Open a Terminal**: Navigate to the directory where you want to create the Angular project.
2. **Create a New Angular Project**: Run the following command:

```bash
Copy code
ng new MyFullStackApp.Frontend
```

1. **Navigate to the Project Directory**: Move into the newly created project folder:

```bash
Copy code
cd MyFullStackApp.Frontend
```

1. **Serve the Angular Application**: Start the development server:

CHAPTER 4: BUILDING YOUR FIRST FULL-STACK APPLICATION

```bash
Copy code
ng serve
```

Your Angular application should now be running at http://localhost:4200.

Step 2: Create the Product Service

To interact with the ASP.NET Core backend from the Angular application, we will create a service that makes HTTP requests to the API.

1. **Generate a Product Service**: Run the following command to generate a new service:

```bash
Copy code
ng generate service product
```

This will create a product.service.ts file in the src/app directory.

1. **Implement the Product Service**: Open product.service.ts and implement the following code:

```typescript
Copy code
import { Injectable } from '@angular/core';
import { HttpClient } from '@angular/common/http';
import { Observable } from 'rxjs';
import { Product } from './product.model';
// Define Product model as needed

@Injectable({
  providedIn: 'root'
})
```

```typescript
export class ProductService {
  private apiUrl = 'http://localhost:5000/api/products'; // API endpoint

  constructor(private http: HttpClient) { }

  getProducts(): Observable<Product[]> {
    return this.http.get<Product[]>(this.apiUrl);
  }

  getProduct(id: number): Observable<Product> {
    return this.http.get<Product>(`${this.apiUrl}/${id}`);
  }

  createProduct(product: Product): Observable<Product> {
    return this.http.post<Product>(this.apiUrl, product);
  }

  updateProduct(product: Product): Observable<void> {
    return this.http.put<void>
(`${this.apiUrl}/${product.id}`, product);
  }

  deleteProduct(id: number): Observable<void> {
    return this.http.delete<void>(`${this.apiUrl}/${id}`);
  }
}
```

In this service:

- We define the API URL pointing to the ASP.NET Core backend.
- We create methods to get, create, update, and delete products using the HttpClient service.

Step 3: Create the Product Model

To ensure type safety, create a model that represents the product.

1. **Generate Product Model**: Create a file named product.model.ts in the

src/app directory.

2. **Define the Product Model**: Open product.model.ts and add the following code:

```typescript
Copy code
export interface Product {
  id: number;
  name: string;
  price: number;
  description: string;
}
```

Step 4: Create the Product Component

Next, we'll create a component to manage products.

1. **Generate Product Component**: Run the following command to create a new component:

```bash
Copy code
ng generate component product
```

1. **Implement the Product Component**: Open product.component.ts and implement the following code:

```typescript
Copy code
import { Component, OnInit } from '@angular/core';
import { ProductService } from '../product.service';
import { Product } from '../product.model';
```

```typescript
@Component({
  selector: 'app-product',
  templateUrl: './product.component.html',
  styleUrls: ['./product.component.css']
})
export class ProductComponent implements OnInit {
  products: Product[] = [];

  constructor(private productService: ProductService) { }

  ngOnInit(): void {
    this.loadProducts();
  }

  loadProducts() {
    this.productService.getProducts().subscribe(data => {
      this.products = data;
    });
  }
}
```

1. **Create Product Component Template**: Open product.component.html and add the following code to display the list of products:

```html
Copy code
<h1>Product List</h1>
<ul>
  <li *ngFor="let product of products">
    {{ product.name }} - {{ product.price | currency }}
  </li>
</ul>
```

1. **Add Routing for Product Component**: If you plan to navigate to this

CHAPTER 4: BUILDING YOUR FIRST FULL-STACK APPLICATION

component, you need to set up routing. Open app-routing.module.ts and add the route for the ProductComponent:

```typescript
Copy code
import { NgModule } from '@angular/core';
import { RouterModule, Routes } from
 '@angular/router';
import { ProductComponent } from
'./product/product.component';

const routes: Routes = [
  { path: 'products', component: ProductComponent },
  { path: '', redirectTo:
'/products', pathMatch: 'full' }
];

@NgModule({
  imports: [RouterModule.forRoot(routes)],
  exports: [RouterModule]
})
export class AppRoutingModule { }
```

1. **Update AppModule**: Ensure that HttpClientModule is imported in your app.module.ts to enable HTTP requests:

```typescript
Copy code
import { HttpClientModule } from '@angular/common/http';

@NgModule({
  declarations: [
    // other components
    ProductComponent
  ],
```

```
  imports: [
    HttpClientModule,
    AppRoutingModule,
    // other modules
  ],
  providers: [],
  bootstrap: [AppComponent]
})
export class AppModule { }
```

Step 5: Test the Angular Application

Now that you have the Angular frontend set up and connected to the ASP.NET Core backend, it's time to test the application.

1. **Run the Angular Application**: Ensure that the ASP.NET Core backend is running. Then, run the Angular application using:

```bash
Copy code
ng serve
```

1. **Open the Browser**: Navigate to http://localhost:4200/products in your browser. You should see the list of products fetched from the ASP.NET Core API.

Deploying Your First Full-Stack App Locally

With both the ASP.NET Core backend and Angular frontend working seamlessly together, it's time to deploy your full-stack application locally. This will allow you to simulate a production-like environment for testing and further development.

Step 1: Prepare the Backend for Deployment

1. **Publish the ASP.NET Core API**: Right-click on the backend project in Visual Studio and select **Publish**. Choose **Folder** as the target and select a folder where you want to publish the API.
2. **Build and Publish**: Click on **Publish** to build and publish the API. This will generate a set of files in the specified folder that can be run independently of Visual Studio.

Step 2: Configure Angular for Production

1. **Build the Angular Application**: Open a terminal in the Angular project folder and run the following command:

```bash
Copy code
ng build --prod
```

This command compiles the Angular application into a production-ready bundle, optimizing it for performance. The output will be located in the dist folder of the Angular project.

Step 3: Serve the Angular Application with ASP.NET Core

To serve the Angular application through the ASP.NET Core backend, you need to configure the Startup.cs file.

1. **Configure Static Files**: In the Startup.cs file of the ASP.NET Core project, modify the Configure method to serve the Angular files:

```csharp
Copy code
public void Configure(IApplicationBuilder app,
    IWebHostEnvironment env)
{
```

```
if (env.IsDevelopment())
{
    app.UseDeveloperExceptionPage();
}
else
{
    app.UseExceptionHandler("/Home/Error");
    app.UseHsts();
}

app.UseHttpsRedirection();
app.UseStaticFiles();

app.UseRouting();

app.UseAuthorization();

app.UseEndpoints(endpoints =>
{
    endpoints.MapControllers();
    endpoints.MapFallbackToFile
("index.html"); // Serve the Angular app
});
}
```

In this code, MapFallbackToFile("index.html") ensures that any unrecognized routes will serve the Angular application's index.html, allowing Angular's routing to take over.

1. **Copy Angular Build Files**: Copy the contents of the dist folder from the Angular project and paste them into the wwwroot folder of the ASP.NET Core project. This allows the ASP.NET Core application to serve the Angular files.

Step 4: Run the Full-Stack Application

1. **Run the ASP.NET Core Application**: Start the ASP.NET Core

application by pressing **F5** in Visual Studio. The application will start and listen for requests.

2. **Access the Application**: Open a web browser and navigate to http://localhost:5000. You should see the Angular application served through the ASP.NET Core backend. You can navigate to /products to view the product list.

Conclusion

In this chapter, we successfully built a full-stack application using ASP.NET Core for the backend and Angular for the frontend. We covered the entire process, including setting up the backend, creating RESTful APIs, connecting the Angular frontend to the backend, and deploying the application locally.

Chapter 5: Working with Data and Databases

I ntroduction

In modern web applications, managing data effectively is crucial for providing a seamless user experience. This chapter focuses on how to work with data in a full-stack application built using ASP.NET Core for the backend and Angular for the frontend. We will explore how to set up a database using Entity Framework Core, perform CRUD operations, and manage relationships between entities. By the end of this chapter, you will have a solid understanding of data management in your full-stack application.

Setting Up a Database with Entity Framework Core

Entity Framework Core (EF Core) is an open-source, lightweight, and extensible version of Entity Framework that works with .NET Core. It provides an Object-Relational Mapping (ORM) framework, allowing developers to work with databases using .NET objects instead of writing raw SQL queries.

1. **Configuring Entity Framework Core**

   To set up EF Core in your ASP.NET Core application, follow these steps:

   1. **Install Required Packages**: Open the **Package Manager Console** in Visual Studio and run the following commands to install EF Core and

CHAPTER 5: WORKING WITH DATA AND DATABASES

SQL Server provider:

```bash
Copy code
Install-Package Microsoft.EntityFrameworkCore
Install-Package Microsoft.EntityFrameworkCore.SqlServer
Install-Package Microsoft.EntityFrameworkCore.Tools
```

1. **Creating the DbContext**: In the **Models** folder, you should have a DbContext class to manage entity objects during runtime. This class is responsible for interacting with the database.

```csharp
Copy code
using Microsoft.EntityFrameworkCore;

namespace MyFullStackApp.Backend.Models
{
    public class ApplicationDbContext : DbContext
    {
        public ApplicationDbContext(DbContextOptions<ApplicationDbContext> options)
            : base(options)
        {
        }

        public DbSet<Product> Products { get; set; }
    }
}
```

1. **Configuring the Connection String**: Update the appsettings.json file to include the connection string for your SQL Server database:

```json
Copy code
{
  "ConnectionStrings": {
    "DefaultConnection":
    "Server=your_server;Database=YourDatabaseName;Trusted_Connection=True;MultipleActiveResultSets=true"
  }
}
```

1. **Registering DbContext in Startup.cs**: In the Startup.cs file, add the DbContext to the service container:

```csharp
Copy code
public void ConfigureServices(IServiceCollection services)
{
    services.AddDbContext<ApplicationDbContext>(options =>
        options.UseSqlServer(Configuration.GetConnectionString("DefaultConnection")));

    services.AddControllers();
    // other services
}
```

2. Creating Migrations

Migrations are a way to update the database schema to match your application's data models. They allow you to version your database changes and apply them systematically.

1. **Enable Migrations**: Open the **Package Manager Console** and run the

following command:

```bash
Copy code
Add-Migration InitialCreate
```

This command creates a new migration class that defines the changes required to create the initial database schema.

1. **Update the Database**: To apply the migration and create the database, run the following command:

```bash
Copy code
Update-Database
```

This command applies any pending migrations to the database, creating tables based on your models.

Performing CRUD Operations

Once the database is set up and the initial migration has been applied, you can start performing CRUD (Create, Read, Update, Delete) operations on your data models.

1. Creating Products

To create products, we will set up an API endpoint that accepts HTTP POST requests. In your ProductsController, implement the following:

```csharp
Copy code
```

```csharp
// POST: api/products
[HttpPost]
public async Task<ActionResult<Product>>
 PostProduct(Product product)
{
    _context.Products.Add(product);
    await _context.SaveChangesAsync();

    return CreatedAtAction(nameof(GetProduct),
 new { id = product.Id }, product);
}
```

This method adds a new product to the database and returns the created product along with a 201 Created status code.

2. Reading Products

To read products, you can implement GET endpoints in your controller:

```csharp
Copy code
// GET: api/products
[HttpGet]
public async Task<ActionResult
<IEnumerable<Product>>> GetProducts()
{
    return await _context.Products.ToListAsync();
}

// GET: api/products/5
[HttpGet("{id}")]
public async Task<ActionResult<Product>> GetProduct(int id)
{
    var product = await _context.Products.FindAsync(id);

    if (product == null)
    {
        return NotFound();
    }
```

CHAPTER 5: WORKING WITH DATA AND DATABASES

```
    return product;
}
```

These methods retrieve a list of all products or a specific product by its ID.

3. Updating Products

To update an existing product, you will need to implement a PUT endpoint:

```csharp
Copy code
// PUT: api/products/5
[HttpPut("{id}")]
public async Task<IActionResult> PutProduct(int id, Product product)
{
    if (id != product.Id)
    {
        return BadRequest();
    }

    _context.Entry(product).State = EntityState.Modified;

    try
    {
        await _context.SaveChangesAsync();
    }
    catch (DbUpdateConcurrencyException)
    {
        if (!ProductExists(id))
        {
            return NotFound();
        }
        else
        {
            throw;
        }
    }

    return NoContent();
```

}

This method updates the product in the database. If the product does not exist, it returns a 404 Not Found response.

4. Deleting Products

To delete a product, implement a DELETE endpoint in your controller:

```csharp
// DELETE: api/products/5
[HttpDelete("{id}")]
public async Task<IActionResult> DeleteProduct(int id)
{
    var product = await _context.Products.FindAsync(id);
    if (product == null)
    {
        return NotFound();
    }

    _context.Products.Remove(product);
    await _context.SaveChangesAsync();

    return NoContent();
}
```

This method removes the specified product from the database.

Managing Relationships Between Entities

In many applications, you will need to manage relationships between different data models. For example, consider an application that includes both Product and Category models, where each product belongs to a category.

1. Defining the Category Model

First, create the Category model in the **Models** folder:

CHAPTER 5: WORKING WITH DATA AND DATABASES

```csharp
Copy code
public class Category
{
    public int Id { get; set; }
    public string Name { get; set; }

    public ICollection<Product> Products { get; set; } = new
    List<Product>();
}
```

This model includes a collection of products associated with the category.

2. Updating the Product Model

Next, update the Product model to include a reference to the Category:

```csharp
Copy code
public class Product
{
    public int Id { get; set; }
    public string Name { get; set; }
    public decimal Price { get; set; }
    public string Description { get; set; }

    public int CategoryId { get; set; }
    public Category Category { get; set; }
}
```

This adds a foreign key relationship between the product and category.

3. Updating the DbContext

Modify the ApplicationDbContext to include the Categories DbSet:

```csharp
Copy code
public DbSet<Category> Categories { get; set; }
```

4. Creating Migrations for Relationships

After updating the models, create a new migration to reflect the changes:

```bash
Copy code
Add-Migration AddCategoryAndProductRelationship
```

Run the following command to update the database:

```bash
Copy code
Update-Database
```

5. Managing Relationships in the API

You can now create API endpoints to manage categories and their associated products. For example, you could implement a method to get all products in a specific category:

```csharp
Copy code
[HttpGet("category/{categoryId}")]
public async Task<ActionResult<IEnumerable<Product>>> GetProductsByCategory(int categoryId)
{
    return await _context.Products.Where(p => p.CategoryId == categoryId).ToListAsync();
}
```

Connecting Angular Frontend to ASP.NET Core Backend

With the backend ready to manage data, we can now connect our Angular frontend to the ASP.NET Core backend to perform CRUD operations on products and categories.

CHAPTER 5: WORKING WITH DATA AND DATABASES

1. Setting Up the Product Service

Modify the existing ProductService to include methods for managing categories. Ensure that your service can handle the API endpoints we've created in the ASP.NET Core backend.

1. **Update the Product Service**: Add methods to get categories and create a new product with a category:

```typescript
Copy code
import { Injectable } from '@angular/core';
import { HttpClient } from '@angular/common/http';
import { Observable } from 'rxjs';
import { Product } from './product.model';
import { Category } from './category.model';

@Injectable({
  providedIn: 'root'
})
export class ProductService {
  private apiUrl = 'http://localhost:5000/api/products'; // API endpoint
  private categoryUrl = 'http://localhost:5000/api/categories';
  // Category API endpoint

  constructor(private http: HttpClient) { }

  getProducts(): Observable<Product[]> {
    return this.http.get<Product[]>(this.apiUrl);
  }

  getCategories(): Observable<Category[]> {
    return this.http.get<Category[]>(this.categoryUrl);
  }
```

```typescript
createProduct(product: Product): 
Observable<Product> {
    return this.http.post<Product>
(this.apiUrl, product);
  }

  // other methods...
}
```

2. Creating the Category Service

Just like we did for the product service, create a new service for managing categories:

1. **Generate Category Service**: Run the following command:

```bash
Copy code
ng generate service category
```

1. **Implement the Category Service**: Open category.service.ts and implement it as follows:

```typescript
Copy code
import { Injectable } from '@angular/core';
import { HttpClient } from '@angular/common/http';
import { Observable } from 'rxjs';
import { Category } from './category.model';

@Injectable({
  providedIn: 'root'
})
```

```
export class CategoryService {
  private categoryUrl = 'http:
//localhost:5000/api/categories';
  // Category API endpoint

  constructor(private http: HttpClient) { }

  getCategories(): Observable<Category[]> {
    return this.http.get
<Category[]>(this.categoryUrl);
  }
}
```

3. Create the Category Model

Create a model for Category in the Angular project:

1. **Create category.model.ts**: In the src/app directory, create a file named category.model.ts:

```typescript
Copy code
export interface Category {
  id: number;
  name: string;
}
```

4. Create the Category Component

Create a component to display and manage categories.

1. **Generate Category Component**: Run the following command:

```bash
Copy code
```

```
ng generate component category
```

1. **Implement the Category Component**: Open category.component.ts and implement it as follows:

```typescript
Copy code
import { Component, OnInit } from '@angular/core';
import { CategoryService } from '../category.service';
import { Category } from '../category.model';

@Component({
  selector: 'app-category',
  templateUrl: './category.component.html',
  styleUrls: ['./category.component.css']
})
export class CategoryComponent implements OnInit {
  categories: Category[] = [];

  constructor(private categoryService: CategoryService) { }

  ngOnInit(): void {
    this.loadCategories();
  }

  loadCategories() {
    this.categoryService.getCategories().subscribe(data => {
      this.categories = data;
    });
  }
}
```

1. **Create Category Component Template**: Open category.component.html and add the following code to display the list of categories:

CHAPTER 5: WORKING WITH DATA AND DATABASES

```html
html
Copy code
<h1>Category List</h1>
<ul>
  <li *ngFor="let category of categories">
    {{ category.name }}
  </li>
</ul>
```

5. Update App Routing

Ensure that your routing is set up to navigate to the new category component:

```typescript
typescript
Copy code
import { NgModule } from '@angular/core';
import { RouterModule, Routes }
 from '@angular/router';
import { ProductComponent }
from './product/product.component';
import { CategoryComponent }
 from './category/category.component';

const routes: Routes = [
  { path: 'products',
component: ProductComponent },
  { path: 'categories',
component: CategoryComponent },
  { path: '', redirectTo:
'/products', pathMatch: 'full' }
];

@NgModule({
  imports: [RouterModule.forRoot(routes)],
  exports: [RouterModule]
})
export class AppRoutingModule { }
```

Deploying Your First Full-Stack App Locally

With the Angular frontend and ASP.NET Core backend set up, it's time to deploy your full-stack application locally for testing and demonstration.

Step 1: Prepare the Backend for Deployment

1. **Publish the ASP.NET Core API**: In Visual Studio, right-click the backend project and select **Publish**. Choose **Folder** as the target and specify a location. Click **Publish** to build the project and generate the deployment files.

Step 2: Build the Angular Application

1. **Build the Angular Application**: In your Angular project folder, run the following command to create a production build:

```bash
Copy code
ng build --prod
```

The output will be generated in the dist folder.

Step 3: Serve Angular with ASP.NET Core

1. **Copy the Angular Build Files**: Copy the contents of the dist folder from the Angular project and paste them into the wwwroot folder of your ASP.NET Core project.
2. **Configure Static File Serving**: Ensure that your Startup.cs is set to serve static files, as previously outlined.

Step 4: Run the Full-Stack Application

1. **Run the ASP.NET Core Application**: Start the ASP.NET Core

application in Visual Studio by pressing **F5**. Ensure that it serves both the API and the Angular frontend.
2. **Open the Application in the Browser**: Navigate to http://localhost:5 000. You should see the Angular application running and able to fetch data from the ASP.NET Core backend.
3. **Test the Application**: Test the CRUD functionality for both products and categories to ensure everything works as expected.

Conclusion

In this chapter, we successfully built our first full-stack application using ASP.NET Core for the backend and Angular for the frontend. We covered setting up a database using Entity Framework Core, performing CRUD operations, managing relationships between entities, and connecting the frontend to the backend.

Chapter 6: Implementing Authentication and Authorization in Your Full-Stack Application

Introduction

In any web application, security is a crucial aspect that cannot be overlooked. Implementing proper authentication and authorization mechanisms is essential for protecting user data and ensuring that only authorized users have access to specific resources. In this chapter, we will explore how to implement authentication and authorization in your full-stack application using ASP.NET Core for the backend and Angular for the frontend.

We will cover the following topics:
1. Understanding Authentication and Authorization
2. Setting Up Identity in ASP.NET Core
3. Creating JWT Tokens for Authentication
4. Implementing Role-Based Authorization
5. Securing API Endpoints
6. Integrating Authentication in Angular
7. Testing Authentication and Authorization

By the end of this chapter, you will have a solid understanding of how to

CHAPTER 6: IMPLEMENTING AUTHENTICATION AND AUTHORIZATION IN...

secure your application and protect sensitive data.

1. Understanding Authentication and Authorization

Before diving into implementation, it's essential to understand the concepts of authentication and authorization.

Authentication

Authentication is the process of verifying the identity of a user or system. It ensures that the user is who they claim to be. In web applications, authentication is typically done through login forms, where users enter their credentials (username and password) to gain access to the application.

Common methods of authentication include:

- **Username and Password**: The most common method, where users provide their credentials to log in.
- **OAuth2**: A protocol that allows third-party applications to obtain limited access to a user's account without exposing their credentials.
- **OpenID Connect**: An identity layer built on top of OAuth2 that provides authentication by allowing clients to verify the identity of users based on the authentication performed by an authorization server.

Authorization

Authorization is the process of determining what an authenticated user is allowed to do within the application. It involves checking the user's permissions and roles to control access to resources.

Common methods of authorization include:

- **Role-Based Access Control (RBAC)**: Users are assigned to specific roles, and each role has defined permissions. This method is straightforward and easy to manage.
- **Claims-Based Authorization**: Users are granted access based on specific claims (attributes or characteristics) associated with their identity.

Understanding these concepts is vital as we build our authentication and authorization system in the full-stack application.

2. Setting Up Identity in ASP.NET Core

ASP.NET Core Identity is a membership system that provides functionality to manage users, passwords, and roles. It simplifies the process of implementing authentication and authorization in ASP.NET Core applications.

Step 1: Install Required Packages

To use ASP.NET Core Identity, you need to install the following NuGet packages:

1. **Open the Package Manager Console** and run the following commands:

```bash
Copy code
Install-Package Microsoft.AspNetCore.Identity.EntityFrameworkCore
Install-Package Microsoft.AspNetCore.Authentication.JwtBearer
```

Step 2: Configure Identity in Startup.cs

In the Startup.cs file, you need to configure Identity services and the authentication middleware.

1. **Add Identity Services**: In the ConfigureServices method, add the following lines to configure Identity:

```csharp
Copy code
```

CHAPTER 6: IMPLEMENTING AUTHENTICATION AND AUTHORIZATION IN...

```csharp
using Microsoft.AspNetCore.Identity;

public void ConfigureServices(IServiceCollection services)
{
    services.AddDbContext<ApplicationDbContext>(options =>
        options.UseSqlServer(Configuration.GetConnectionString("DefaultConnection")));

    services.AddIdentity<IdentityUser, IdentityRole>()
        .AddEntityFrameworkStores<ApplicationDbContext>()
        .AddDefaultTokenProviders();

    services.AddControllers();
    services.AddSwaggerGen();
    // Other services...
}
```

This code configures ASP.NET Core Identity to use Entity Framework Core with the ApplicationDbContext.

1. **Configure Authentication Middleware**: In the Configure method, add the JWT Bearer authentication middleware:

```
csharp
Copy code
using Microsoft.AspNetCore.Authentication.JwtBearer;

public void Configure(IApplicationBuilder app, IWebHostEnvironment env)
{
    // Other middleware...

    app.UseAuthentication();
    app.UseAuthorization();

    app.UseEndpoints(endpoints =>
    {
```

```
            endpoints.MapControllers();
            endpoints.MapFallbackToFile("index.html");
    });
}
```

Step 3: Create a User Registration and Login API

Now that Identity is set up, let's create API endpoints for user registration and login.

1. **Create an AuthController**: In the **Controllers** folder, create a new controller named AuthController.cs:

```csharp
Copy code
using Microsoft.AspNetCore.Identity;
using Microsoft.AspNetCore.Mvc;
using Microsoft.IdentityModel.Tokens;
using System.IdentityModel.Tokens.Jwt;
using System.Security.Claims;
using System.Text;
using System.Threading.Tasks;

namespace MyFullStackApp.Backend.Controllers
{
    [Route("api/[controller]")]
    [ApiController]
    public class AuthController : ControllerBase
    {
        private readonly UserManager<IdentityUser> _userManager;
        private readonly SignInManager<IdentityUser> _signInManager;
        private readonly IConfiguration _configuration;

        public AuthController(UserManager
```

CHAPTER 6: IMPLEMENTING AUTHENTICATION AND AUTHORIZATION IN...

```
<IdentityUser> userManager,
SignInManager<IdentityUser>
signInManager, IConfiguration configuration)
        {
            _userManager = userManager;
            _signInManager = signInManager;
            _configuration = configuration;
        }

        // POST: api/auth/register
        [HttpPost("register")]
        public async Task<IActionResult>
 Register([FromBody]
UserRegistrationDto registrationDto)
        {
var user = new IdentityUser
{ UserName = registrationDto.
Email, Email = registrationDto.Email };
var result = await _
userManager.CreateAsync
(user, registrationDto.Password);

            if (result.Succeeded)
            {
                return Ok();
            }

            return BadRequest(result.Errors);
        }

        // POST: api/auth/login
        [HttpPost("login")]
        public async Task<
IActionResult> Login([FromBody]
 UserLoginDto loginDto)
        {
var result = await _
signInManager.PasswordSignInAsync
(loginDto.Email, loginDto.Password, false, false);
if (result.Succeeded)
```

```csharp
            {
                var user = await
                _userManager.FindByEmailAsync(loginDto.Email);
var token = GenerateJwtToken(user);
return Ok(new { Token = token });
            }

            return Unauthorized();
        }

private string GenerateJwtToken
(IdentityUser user)
        {
            var claims = new[]
            {
new Claim(JwtRegisteredClaimNames.
Sub, user.UserName),
new Claim(JwtRegistered
ClaimNames.Jti, user.Id)
            };

var key = new
SymmetricSecurityKey(Encoding.
UTF8.GetBytes(_configuration["Jwt:Key"]));
var creds = new SigningCredentials(key,
SecurityAlgorithms.HmacSha256);

var token = new JwtSecurityToken(
issuer: _configuration["Jwt:Issuer"],
audience: _configuration["Jwt:Audience"],
claims: claims,
expires: DateTime.Now.AddMinutes(30),
signingCredentials: creds);

return new JwtSecurityTokenHandler().
WriteToken(token);
        }
    }
}
```

In this code:

CHAPTER 6: IMPLEMENTING AUTHENTICATION AND AUTHORIZATION IN...

- We create an API endpoint for user registration (/api/auth/register) and user login (/api/auth/login).
- The GenerateJwtToken method creates a JWT token for the authenticated user.

Step 4: Create DTOs for Registration and Login

To handle registration and login requests, create two Data Transfer Objects (DTOs).

1. **Create a UserRegistrationDto Class**: In the **Models** folder, create a class named UserRegistrationDto.cs:

```csharp
Copy code
public class UserRegistrationDto
{
    public string Email { get; set; }
    public string Password { get; set; }
}
```

1. **Create a UserLoginDto Class**: In the **Models** folder, create a class named UserLoginDto.cs:

```csharp
Copy code
public class UserLoginDto
{
    public string Email { get; set; }
    public string Password { get; set; }
}
```

3. Creating JWT Tokens for Authentication

JSON Web Tokens (JWT) are an open standard (RFC 7519) for securely transmitting information between parties as a JSON object. They are commonly used for authentication and information exchange.

Step 1: Configure JWT in appsettings.json

To use JWT in your application, you need to configure the JWT settings in the appsettings.json file:

```json
Copy code
{
  "Jwt": {
    "Key": "Your_Secret_Key_Here",
// Change this to a strong secret key
    "Issuer": "MyFullStackApp",
    "Audience": "MyFullStackAppUsers"
  }
}
```

Make sure to use a strong, randomly generated secret key for production applications.

Step 2: Configure JWT Authentication in Startup.cs

In the ConfigureServices method of Startup.cs, add the JWT authentication services:

```csharp
Copy code
using Microsoft.AspNetCore.Authentication.JwtBearer;
using Microsoft.IdentityModel.Tokens;

public void ConfigureServices
(IServiceCollection services)
{
    // Other configurations...
```

CHAPTER 6: IMPLEMENTING AUTHENTICATION AND AUTHORIZATION IN...

```
    var key = Encoding.UTF8.GetBytes
(Configuration["Jwt:Key"]);
    services.AddAuthentication(options =>
    {
        options.DefaultAuthenticateScheme =
        JwtBearerDefaults.AuthenticationScheme;
        options.DefaultChallengeScheme =
        JwtBearerDefaults.AuthenticationScheme;
    })
    .AddJwtBearer(options =>
    {
        options.TokenValidationParameters = new
        TokenValidationParameters
        {
ValidateIssuer = true,
ValidateAudience = true,
ValidateLifetime = true,
ValidateIssuerSigningKey = true,
ValidIssuer = Configuration["Jwt:Issuer"],
ValidAudience = Configuration["Jwt:Audience"],
IssuerSigningKey = new SymmetricSecurityKey(key)
        };
    });
}
```

This code configures JWT authentication, specifying how tokens should be validated.

Step 3: Protecting API Endpoints

To protect specific API endpoints and require authentication, you can use the [Authorize] attribute.

For example, to protect the ProductsController, modify it as follows:

```
csharp
Copy code
using Microsoft.AspNetCore.Authorization;

[Authorize]
```

```csharp
[Route("api/[controller]")]
[ApiController]
public class ProductsController : ControllerBase
{
    // Existing code...
}
```

Now, only authenticated users with a valid JWT token can access the endpoints in this controller.

4. Implementing Role-Based Authorization

Role-based authorization allows you to define roles and restrict access to certain resources based on the user's role.

Step 1: Create Roles in ASP.NET Core Identity

1. **Create a Role Model**: First, ensure your application supports roles by adding the necessary using directives in Startup.cs:

```csharp
Copy code
using Microsoft.AspNetCore.Identity;
```

1. **Seed Roles in the Database**: You can seed roles during the application startup. In the Configure method of Startup.cs, add the following code:

```csharp
Copy code
private async Task CreateRoles
(IServiceProvider serviceProvider)
{
```

CHAPTER 6: IMPLEMENTING AUTHENTICATION AND AUTHORIZATION IN...

```csharp
    var roleManager = serviceProvider.GetRequiredService<RoleManager<IdentityRole>>();

    string[] roleNames = { "Admin", "User" };

    foreach (var roleName in roleNames)
    {
        var roleExist = await roleManager.RoleExistsAsync(roleName);
        if (!roleExist)
        {
            await roleManager.CreateAsync(new IdentityRole(roleName));
        }
    }
}
```

Call this method within the Configure method:

csharp
Copy code
```csharp
public void Configure(IApplicationBuilder
  app, IWebHostEnvironment env, IServiceProvider serviceProvider)
{
    // Other configurations...

    CreateRoles(serviceProvider).Wait();
}
```

Step 2: Assign Roles to Users

You can assign roles to users during registration or from an admin panel.

To assign a role during registration, modify the Register method in the AuthController:

csharp
Copy code

```csharp
[HttpPost("register")]
public async Task<IActionResult> Register([FromBody] 
UserRegistrationDto registrationDto)
{
    var user = new IdentityUser
{ UserName = registrationDto.Email, 
Email = registrationDto.Email };
    var result = await _userManager.CreateAsync(user, 
    registrationDto.Password);

    if (result.Succeeded)
    {
        await _userManager.
AddToRoleAsync(user, "User"); // Assign default role
        return Ok();
    }

    return BadRequest(result.Errors);
}
```

Step 3: Protect Routes Based on Roles

To restrict access to specific routes based on roles, use the [Authorize] attribute with the Roles parameter:

```
csharp
Copy code
[Authorize(Roles = "Admin")]
[HttpPost("create")]
public async Task<IActionResult> 
  CreateProduct(Product product)
{
    // Method implementation...
}
```

This ensures that only users with the "Admin" role can access the CreateProduct endpoint.

CHAPTER 6: IMPLEMENTING AUTHENTICATION AND AUTHORIZATION IN...

5. *Securing API Endpoints*

To ensure the security of your API endpoints, implement the following best practices:

Step 1: Use HTTPS

Always use HTTPS to encrypt data in transit. Ensure your application is configured to redirect HTTP requests to HTTPS:

```csharp
Copy code
app.UseHttpsRedirection();
```

Step 2: Validate Input Data

Always validate input data to prevent injection attacks. Use data annotations in your model classes to enforce validation rules.

Example of input validation:

```csharp
Copy code
public class Product
{
    public int Id { get; set; }

    [Required]
    public string Name { get; set; }

    [Range(0.01, double.MaxValue,
ErrorMessage = "Price must be greater than zero.")]
    public decimal Price { get; set; }

    public string Description { get; set; }
}
```

Step 3: Rate Limiting

Implement rate limiting to protect your API from abuse. This can be achieved using middleware or by configuring your API gateway.

Step 4: Logging and Monitoring

Implement logging to monitor access attempts and any suspicious activity. Use built-in logging features in ASP.NET Core or integrate third-party logging libraries.

6. Integrating Authentication in Angular

Now that we have set up authentication in the backend, it's time to integrate it into the Angular frontend.

Step 1: Install Angular JWT Package

To handle JWT tokens in Angular, install the @auth0/angular-jwt package:

```bash
Copy code
npm install @auth0/angular-jwt
```

Step 2: Create an Auth Service

Create an AuthService to manage authentication in your Angular application.

1. **Generate Auth Service**: Run the following command:

```bash
Copy code
ng generate service auth
```

1. **Implement the Auth Service**: Open auth.service.ts and implement the following code:

CHAPTER 6: IMPLEMENTING AUTHENTICATION AND AUTHORIZATION IN...

```typescript
Copy code
import { Injectable } from '@angular/core';
import { HttpClient } from '@angular/common/http';
import { BehaviorSubject, Observable } from 'rxjs';
import { Router } from '@angular/router';

@Injectable({
  providedIn: 'root'
})
export class AuthService {
  private apiUrl = 'http://localhost:5000/api/auth';
  private token: string | null = null;
  private isLoggedInSubject: BehaviorSubject<boolean> = new BehaviorSubject<boolean>(false);

  constructor(private http: HttpClient, private router: Router) {
    this.token = localStorage.getItem('token');
    this.isLoggedInSubject.next(!!this.token);
  }

  register(user: { email: string, password: string }): Observable<any> {
    return this.http.post(`${this.apiUrl}/register`, user);
  }

  login(user: { email: string, password: string }): Observable<any> {
    return this.http.post(`${this.apiUrl}/login`, user);
  }

  logout() {
    localStorage.removeItem('token');
    this.token = null;
    this.isLoggedInSubject.next(false);
    this.router.navigate(['/login']);
// Redirect to login
```

```
  }

  isLoggedIn(): Observable<boolean> {
    return this.isLoggedInSubject.asObservable();
  }
}
```

This service handles registration, login, and logout functionalities. It also tracks the user's login status.

Step 3: Implement Authentication Guards

Authentication guards can protect routes in your Angular application, ensuring that only logged-in users can access certain areas.

1. **Generate Auth Guard**: Run the following command:

```bash
Copy code
ng generate guard auth
```

1. **Implement Auth Guard**: Open auth.guard.ts and implement the following code:

```typescript
Copy code
import { Injectable } from '@angular/core';
import { CanActivate, ActivatedRouteSnapshot,
 RouterStateSnapshot, Router }
 from '@angular/router';
import { AuthService } from './auth.service';
import { Observable } from 'rxjs';

@Injectable({
```

CHAPTER 6: IMPLEMENTING AUTHENTICATION AND AUTHORIZATION IN...

```
    providedIn: 'root'
})
export class AuthGuard implements CanActivate {
    constructor(private authService:
AuthService, private router: Router) {}

    canActivate(
        next: ActivatedRouteSnapshot,
        state: RouterStateSnapshot):
Observable<boolean> |
Promise<boolean> | boolean {
        return this.authService.
isLoggedIn().pipe(
            map(isLoggedIn => {
                if (!isLoggedIn) {
this.router.navigate
(['/login']); // Redirect to login
                    return false;
                }
                return true;
            })
        );
    }
}
```

This guard checks the user's login status and redirects them to the login page if they are not authenticated.

Step 4: Create Login and Registration Components

Create components for user login and registration.

1. **Generate Login Component**: Run the following command:

```bash
Copy code
ng generate component login
```

1. **Implement Login Component**: Open login.component.ts and implement the following code:

```typescript
import { Component } from '@angular/core';
import { FormBuilder, FormGroup, Validators } from '@angular/forms';
import { AuthService } from '../auth.service';
import { Router } from '@angular/router';

@Component({
  selector: 'app-login',
  templateUrl: './login.component.html',
})
export class LoginComponent {
  loginForm: FormGroup;

  constructor(private fb: FormBuilder, private authService: AuthService, private router: Router) {
    this.loginForm = this.fb.group({
      email: ['', [Validators.required, Validators.email]],
      password: ['', [Validators.required]]
    });
  }

  onSubmit() {
    if (this.loginForm.valid) {
      this.authService.login(this.loginForm.value).subscribe(
        response => {
          localStorage.setItem('token', response.token);
          this.router.navigate(['/products']);
        },
```

CHAPTER 6: IMPLEMENTING AUTHENTICATION AND AUTHORIZATION IN...

```
      error => {
        console.error('Login failed', error);
      }
    );
  }
 }
}
```

1. **Create Login Component Template**: Open login.component.html and add the following code:

```html
Copy code
<form [formGroup]="loginForm" (ngSubmit)="onSubmit()">
  <label for="email">Email:</label>
  <input id="email" formControlName="email">
  <div *ngIf="loginForm.get('email')?.invalid && 
  loginForm.get('email')?.touched">Invalid email.</div>

  <label for="password">Password:</label>
  <input id="password" type=
"password" formControlName="password">
  <div *ngIf="loginForm.get('password')?.invalid && 
  loginForm.get('password')?.
touched">Password is required.</div>

  <button type="submit" [disabled]=
"loginForm.invalid">Login</button>
</form>
```

Step 5: Create Registration Component

1. **Generate Registration Component**: Run the following command:

```bash
Copy code
ng generate component register
```

1. **Implement Registration Component**: Open register.component.ts and implement the following code:

```typescript
Copy code
import { Component } from '@angular/core';
import { FormBuilder, FormGroup, Validators } from '@angular/forms';
import { AuthService } from '../auth.service';
import { Router } from '@angular/router';

@Component({
  selector: 'app-register',
  templateUrl: './register.component.html',
})
export class RegisterComponent {
  registrationForm: FormGroup;

  constructor(private fb: FormBuilder,
 private authService: AuthService, private router: Router) {
    this.registrationForm = this.fb.group({
      email: ['', [Validators.required, Validators.email]],
      password: ['', [Validators.required]]
    });
  }

  onSubmit() {
    if (this.registrationForm.valid) {
      this.authService.register(this.registrationForm.value).subscribe(
        () => {
```

CHAPTER 6: IMPLEMENTING AUTHENTICATION AND AUTHORIZATION IN...

```
            this.router.navigate(['/login']);
        },
        error => {
            console.error('Registration failed', error);
        }
      );
   }
  }
}
```

1. **Create Registration Component Template**: Open register.compone nt.html and add the following code:

html
Copy code
```
<form [formGroup]="registrationForm"
(ngSubmit)="onSubmit()">
  <label for="email">Email:</label>
  <input id="email" formControlName="email">
  <div *ngIf="registrationForm.get
('email')?.invalid && registrationForm.get('email')?.
touched">Invalid email.</div>

  <label for="password">Password:</label>
  <input id="password" type="password"
formControlName="password">
  <div *ngIf="registrationForm.
get('password')?.invalid &&
registrationForm.get('password')?.
touched">Password is required.</div>

  <button type="submit" [disabled]=
"registrationForm.invalid">
Register</button>
</form>
```

7. Testing Authentication and Authorization

Now that we have integrated authentication and authorization into our application, it's time to test everything to ensure it works as expected.

Step 1: Testing User Registration and Login

1. **Run the ASP.NET Core Backend**: Start your ASP.NET Core application to ensure the API is running.
2. **Run the Angular Frontend**: Start the Angular application in a separate terminal.
3. **Register a New User**: Navigate to the registration page and create a new user. Verify that the user is created successfully.
4. **Login with the New User**: Navigate to the login page, enter the credentials of the newly created user, and check if you are redirected to the products page.

Step 2: Testing Protected Routes

1. **Access Protected Routes**: Attempt to access a protected route (e.g., /products) without logging in. You should be redirected to the login page.
2. **Access Protected Routes After Logging In**: After logging in, try accessing the protected route again. Verify that you can access the page without being redirected.

Step 3: Test Role-Based Authorization

If you have implemented role-based authorization, test it by creating users with different roles and ensuring that only authorized users can access specific routes.

Conclusion

In this chapter, we successfully implemented authentication and authorization in our full-stack application using ASP.NET Core and Angular. We covered the setup of ASP.NET Core Identity, JWT token generation, role-based authorization, and integrating these features into the Angular frontend.

Chapter 7: Error Handling and Validation in Your Full-Stack Application

Introduction

In any application, handling errors gracefully and validating user input are crucial aspects of providing a seamless user experience. Users should be informed about what went wrong when an error occurs and what data is expected from them when filling out forms. This chapter will delve into error handling and validation strategies for both the backend (ASP.NET Core) and frontend (Angular) of your full-stack application.

We will cover the following topics:
1. Understanding Error Handling
2. Implementing Global Error Handling in ASP.NET Core
3. Validating User Input in ASP.NET Core
4. Error Handling in Angular
5. Form Validation in Angular
6. Implementing User-Friendly Error Messages
7. Testing Error Handling and Validation

By the end of this chapter, you will have a robust understanding of how to handle errors and validate data effectively in your application.

1. Understanding Error Handling

Error handling refers to the process of responding to and managing errors that occur during the execution of an application. Proper error handling allows developers to:

- Identify and log errors for debugging purposes.
- Provide users with meaningful feedback when something goes wrong.
- Prevent application crashes and unexpected behavior.

Errors can occur for various reasons, including invalid user input, network issues, server failures, and more. It's essential to design your application to handle these errors gracefully.

2. Implementing Global Error Handling in ASP.NET Core

ASP.NET Core provides a middleware pipeline that allows developers to implement global error handling. This approach centralizes error handling and ensures that all errors are logged and managed consistently.

Step 1: Use Exception Handling Middleware

In the Startup.cs file, configure exception handling middleware in the Configure method:

```csharp
csharp
Copy code
public void Configure(IApplicationBuilder app, IWebHostEnvironment env)
{
    if (env.IsDevelopment())
    {
        app.UseDeveloperExceptionPage();
    }
    else
    {
```

```
        app.UseExceptionHandler("/api/error");
        app.UseHsts();
    }

    app.UseHttpsRedirection();
    app.UseRouting();
    app.UseAuthentication();
    app.UseAuthorization();
    app.UseEndpoints(endpoints =>
    {
        endpoints.MapControllers();
    });
}
```

In this code:

- UseExceptionHandler("/api/error") specifies a custom error handling route for production environments.

Step 2: Create an Error Controller

To handle errors, create an ErrorController in the **Controllers** folder:

```csharp
Copy code
using Microsoft.AspNetCore.Mvc;

namespace MyFullStackApp.Backend.Controllers
{
    [Route("api/[controller]")]
    [ApiController]
    public class ErrorController : ControllerBase
    {
        [HttpGet]
        public IActionResult HandleError()
        {
            return Problem("An error occurred while processing your request.");
```

CHAPTER 7: ERROR HANDLING AND VALIDATION IN YOUR FULL-STACK...

```
        }
    }
}
```

This controller provides a simple error response that can be customized further.

Step 3: Logging Errors

Logging errors is essential for debugging and monitoring application performance. You can use built-in logging providers in ASP.NET Core.

1. **Configure Logging in Startup.cs**: In the ConfigureServices method, add logging services:

```csharp
Copy code
public void ConfigureServices(IServiceCollection services)
{
    services.AddLogging();
    // other services
}
```

1. **Log Errors in ErrorController**: Modify the ErrorController to log errors:

```csharp
Copy code
using Microsoft.Extensions.Logging;

public class ErrorController : ControllerBase
{
    private readonly ILogger<ErrorController> _logger;
```

```csharp
public ErrorController(ILogger<ErrorController> logger)
{
    _logger = logger;
}

[HttpGet]
public IActionResult HandleError()
{
    _logger.LogError("An error occurred while processing the request.");
    return Problem("An error occurred while processing your request.");
}
}
```

3. Validating User Input in ASP.NET Core

Input validation is critical to ensuring data integrity and protecting your application from malicious input. ASP.NET Core provides built-in validation mechanisms through data annotations.

Step 1: Use Data Annotations for Validation

Data annotations are attributes that you can apply to model properties to enforce validation rules.

1. **Add Validation Attributes to Models**: Update your Product model to include validation:

csharp
Copy code
```
using System.ComponentModel.DataAnnotations;

public class Product
{
```

CHAPTER 7: ERROR HANDLING AND VALIDATION IN YOUR FULL-STACK...

```csharp
    public int Id { get; set; }

    [Required(ErrorMessage = "Name is required.")]
    public string Name { get; set; }

    [Required(ErrorMessage = "Price is required.")]
    [Range(0.01, double.MaxValue,
 ErrorMessage = "Price must be greater than zero.")]
    public decimal Price { get; set; }

    public string Description { get; set; }
}
```

In this example, the Name property is marked as required, and the Price property has a range constraint.

Step 2: Validate Input in Controller Actions

In your ProductsController, validate input data automatically:

```csharp
Copy code
[HttpPost]
public async Task<ActionResult<Product>>
 PostProduct([FromBody] Product product)
{
    if (!ModelState.IsValid)
    {
        return BadRequest(ModelState);
    }

    _context.Products.Add(product);
    await _context.SaveChangesAsync();

    return CreatedAtAction(nameof(GetProduct),
 new { id = product.Id }, product);
}
```

The ModelState.IsValid property checks whether the incoming model passes validation. If it fails, a 400 Bad Request response is returned with the validation errors.

4. Error Handling in Angular

Handling errors in the Angular frontend is equally important. Users should receive clear messages when something goes wrong, such as when an API call fails.

Step 1: Create an Error Handling Service
To centralize error handling in Angular, create a service.

1. **Generate an Error Handling Service**: Run the following command:

```bash
Copy code
ng generate service error
```

1. **Implement the Error Handling Service**: Open error.service.ts and implement it as follows:

```typescript
Copy code
import { Injectable } from '@angular/core';
import { HttpErrorResponse } from '@angular/common/http';
import { MatSnackBar } from '@angular/material/snack-bar';

@Injectable({
  providedIn: 'root'
})
export class ErrorService {
  constructor(private snackBar: MatSnackBar) {}
```

```
  handleError(error: HttpErrorResponse) {
    let errorMessage = 'An unknown error occurred!';

    if (error.error instanceof ErrorEvent) {
      // Client-side error
      errorMessage = `Error: ${error.error.message}`;
    } else {
      // Server-side error
      errorMessage = `Error ${error.status}: ${error.message}`;
    }

    this.snackBar.open(errorMessage, 'Close', {
      duration: 5000,
    });
  }
}
```

This service uses Angular Material's Snackbar to display error messages.

Step 2: Handle Errors in Services

In your services, call the ErrorService when an error occurs:

```typescript
Copy code
import { Injectable } from '@angular/core';
import { HttpClient } from '@angular/common/http';
import { Product } from './product.model';
import { ErrorService } from './error.service';
import { Observable } from 'rxjs';
import { catchError } from 'rxjs/operators';

@Injectable({
  providedIn: 'root'
})
export class ProductService {
  private apiUrl = 'http://localhost:5000/api/products';
```

```
constructor(private http: HttpClient,
private errorService: ErrorService) { }

  getProducts(): Observable<Product[]> {
    return this.http.get<Product[]>(this.apiUrl).pipe(
      catchError(error => {
        this.errorService.handleError(error);
        throw error;
      })
    );
  }

  // Other methods...
}
```

By using the catchError operator, we can catch errors and handle them accordingly.

5. Form Validation in Angular

Validating user input on the frontend is essential for enhancing user experience and preventing invalid data from being submitted to the server.

Step 1: Implement Reactive Forms

Angular provides a powerful reactive forms module that allows for complex form validations.

1. **Import ReactiveFormsModule**: In your app.module.ts, import ReactiveFormsModule:

```typescript
Copy code
import { ReactiveFormsModule } from '@angular/forms';

@NgModule({
```

CHAPTER 7: ERROR HANDLING AND VALIDATION IN YOUR FULL-STACK...

```
  imports: [
    ReactiveFormsModule,
    // Other imports...
  ],
})
export class AppModule { }
```

1. **Create a Form in the Component**: In your product component, implement a reactive form for product creation:

```typescript
Copy code
import { Component, OnInit } from '@angular/core';
import { FormBuilder, FormGroup, Validators } from '@angular/forms';
import { ProductService } from '../product.service';

@Component({
  selector: 'app-product-create',
  templateUrl: './product-create.component.html',
})
export class ProductCreateComponent
implements OnInit {
  productForm: FormGroup;

  constructor(private fb: FormBuilder,
 private productService: ProductService) {
    this.productForm = this.fb.group({
      name: ['', Validators.required],
      price: ['', [Validators.required,
Validators.min(0.01)]],
      description: ['']
    });
  }

  ngOnInit(): void {}
```

```
onSubmit() {
  if (this.productForm.valid) {
    this.productService.createProduct
(this.productForm.value).subscribe(
      response => {
        // Handle success
      },
      error => {
        // Handle error
      }
    );
  } else {
    // Show validation errors
  }
}
}
```

1. **Create Product Create Template**: In product-create.component.html, create the form template:

html
Copy code
```
<form [formGroup]="productForm"
```

Chapter 8: Enhancing User Experience with UI/UX Design Principles

Introduction

User experience (UX) and user interface (UI) design are critical aspects of any web application. A well-designed application not only looks good but also provides a seamless and intuitive experience for users. In this chapter, we will explore essential UI/UX design principles and how to implement them in your full-stack application built with ASP.NET Core and Angular.

We will cover the following topics:
1. Understanding UI and UX
2. Key Principles of UI/UX Design
3. Implementing Responsive Design
4. Enhancing Navigation and Accessibility
5. Leveraging Angular Material for UI Components
6. Best Practices for Form Design
7. User Testing and Feedback

By the end of this chapter, you will have a comprehensive understanding of how to enhance user experience through effective UI/UX design.

1. Understanding UI and UX

User Interface (UI) refers to the visual elements of an application that users interact with, such as buttons, forms, and navigation menus. It encompasses everything from the layout and colors to typography and spacing.

User Experience (UX), on the other hand, refers to the overall experience a user has while interacting with an application. This includes usability, accessibility, performance, and how the application meets user needs and expectations.

While UI focuses on the aesthetic and interactive elements, UX emphasizes the user's journey and satisfaction with the application. Both UI and UX are interconnected, and good design requires a balance of both.

2. Key Principles of UI/UX Design

2.1. Consistency

Consistency in design helps users understand how to interact with your application. It involves using the same elements and behaviors throughout the application.

- **Visual Consistency**: Maintain uniformity in color schemes, fonts, and layout across different pages and components.
- **Functional Consistency**: Ensure that similar actions produce similar results. For example, if a button is used for saving in one part of the application, it should function the same way in other parts.

2.2. Simplicity

Simplicity is a cornerstone of effective UI/UX design. Users should be able to navigate and interact with your application without feeling overwhelmed.

- **Minimalist Design**: Use a clean and uncluttered layout. Remove unnecessary elements that do not contribute to the user's primary tasks.
- **Clear Language**: Use simple and concise language in buttons, labels, and

instructions.

2.3. Feedback

Providing feedback is essential for informing users about the results of their actions. This can include visual cues, animations, and messages.

- **Visual Feedback**: Use hover effects, loading indicators, and confirmation messages to inform users of their actions.
- **Error Messages**: Display clear and specific error messages when user input fails validation.

2.4. Hierarchy

Designing a clear visual hierarchy helps users understand the importance of different elements within the interface.

- **Size and Color**: Use size, color, and contrast to draw attention to important elements such as call-to-action buttons.
- **Grouping**: Group related items together and use whitespace effectively to separate different sections.

3. Implementing Responsive Design

Responsive design ensures that your application looks and functions well on various devices and screen sizes. With the increasing use of mobile devices, it's essential to implement a responsive layout.

3.1. CSS Media Queries

CSS media queries allow you to apply styles based on the screen size or device type. Use them to create breakpoints for different layouts:

```css
Copy code
/* Styles for mobile devices */
@media (max-width: 600px) {
```

```css
  .container {
    flex-direction: column;
  }
}

/* Styles for tablets and larger devices */
@media (min-width: 601px) {
  .container {
    flex-direction: row;
  }
}
```

3.2. Flexbox and Grid Layouts

CSS Flexbox and Grid are powerful layout systems that help create responsive designs with ease.

- **Flexbox**: Ideal for one-dimensional layouts (rows or columns).

```css
Copy code
.container {
  display: flex;
  justify-content: space-between;
}
```

- **Grid**: Suitable for two-dimensional layouts (both rows and columns).

```css
Copy code
.container {
  display: grid;
  grid-template-columns: repeat(3, 1fr);
}
```

3.3. Mobile-First Design

Start by designing for the smallest screen sizes first and progressively enhance the layout for larger screens. This approach ensures a better experience on mobile devices.

1. **Define Styles for Mobile**: Write CSS rules targeting mobile devices first.
2. **Use Media Queries for Larger Screens**: Add media queries to adjust the layout for tablets and desktops.

4. Enhancing Navigation and Accessibility

A well-structured navigation system is crucial for helping users find what they need. Additionally, accessibility ensures that all users, including those with disabilities, can interact with your application.

4.1. Navigation Design

1. **Use a Clear Navigation Bar**: Ensure the navigation bar is easy to locate and understand. Use clear labels and consider including dropdown menus for subcategories.
2. **Implement Breadcrumbs**: Breadcrumbs provide users with a trail to follow back to the previous pages. They help users understand their location within the application.

```html
html
Copy code
<nav>
  <ul class="breadcrumb">
    <li><a href="/">Home</a></li>
    <li><a href="/products">Products</a></li>
    <li>Product Details</li>
  </ul>
</nav>
```

4.2. Accessibility Features

1. **Semantic HTML**: Use semantic HTML elements (e.g., <header>, <nav>, <main>, <footer>) to enhance accessibility. This helps screen readers understand the structure of your page.
2. **Alt Text for Images**: Always provide descriptive alt text for images to assist visually impaired users:

```html
Copy code
<img src="logo.png" alt="Company Logo">
```

1. **Keyboard Navigation**: Ensure that users can navigate the application using a keyboard. This involves using appropriate tabindex attributes and focus management.
2. **Contrast and Readability**: Ensure sufficient contrast between text and background colors to improve readability. Use tools like the WebAIM Contrast Checker to verify accessibility standards.

5. *Leveraging Angular Material for UI Components*

Angular Material is a UI component library for Angular applications that implements Google's Material Design. It provides pre-built components that adhere to best practices in UI design.

5.1. Installing Angular Material

To use Angular Material in your application, install the library using the Angular CLI:

```bash
Copy code
```

CHAPTER 8: ENHANCING USER EXPERIENCE WITH UI/UX DESIGN...

```
ng add @angular/material
```

This command sets up Angular Material in your project and allows you to choose a theme.

5.2. Using Material Components

Once Angular Material is installed, you can start using its components. Here are some commonly used components:

1. **Buttons**: Use Material buttons for consistent styling.

```html
Copy code
<button mat-button (click)="onAddProduct()">Add Product</button>
```

1. **Input Fields**: Use Material input fields for better form styling and validation.

```html
Copy code
<mat-form-field>
  <input matInput placeholder="Product Name" formControlName="name" required>
  <mat-error *ngIf="productForm.get('name').hasError('required')">Name is required.</mat-error>
</mat-form-field>
```

1. **Snack Bar for Notifications**: Use Angular Material's Snackbar for displaying notifications or error messages.

```typescript
Copy code
this.snackBar.open('Product created successfully!', 'Close', {
  duration: 3000,
});
```

1. **Dialog for Confirmations**: Use dialogs for confirming actions, such as deleting a product.

```typescript
Copy code
const dialogRef = this.dialog.open(ConfirmDialogComponent);
dialogRef.afterClosed().subscribe(result => {
  if (result) {
    // Proceed with the action
  }
});
```

5.3. Theming with Angular Material

You can customize the look and feel of your Angular Material components by defining your own themes. You can choose between a light theme, dark theme, or create a custom theme.

1. **Create a Theme**: In your styles file (e.g., styles.scss), define your theme:

```scss
Copy code
@import '~@angular/material/theming';
@include mat-core();

$primary: mat-palette($mat-indigo);
```

```
$accent: mat-palette($mat-pink);
$theme: mat-light-theme($primary, $accent);

@include angular-material-theme($theme);
```

1. **Apply the Theme**: The theme will automatically apply to all Angular Material components in your application.

6. Best Practices for Form Design

Forms are a crucial part of web applications, and well-designed forms enhance user experience and data integrity.

6.1. Keep Forms Simple

1. **Limit the Number of Fields**: Only include necessary fields in the form. The more fields a user has to fill out, the less likely they are to complete the form.
2. **Use Grouping and Sections**: Group related fields together to help users navigate the form more easily.

6.2. Provide Clear Labels and Instructions

1. **Use Descriptive Labels**: Ensure labels clearly describe the input field's purpose. Use placeholders sparingly, as they can be easily forgotten.

```html
Copy code
<label for="email">Email Address</label>
<input type="email" id="email" name="email" required>
```

1. **Include Help Text**: Provide additional context or instructions for fields

that may require clarification.

6.3. Implement Validation and Feedback

1. **Immediate Feedback**: Provide immediate feedback for validation errors as users fill out the form. Use visual indicators (e.g., red outlines) and error messages.

```html
Copy code
<mat-form-field>
  <input matInput placeholder="Email" formControlName="email" required>
  <mat-error *ngIf="form.get('email').hasError('required')">Email is required.</mat-error>
</mat-form-field>
```

1. **Confirmation Messages**: After a successful form submission, provide a confirmation message to inform users of the outcome.

7. User Testing and Feedback

Gathering user feedback and conducting usability testing are vital for improving your application's design and functionality.

7.1. Conducting Usability Testing

Usability testing involves observing real users as they interact with your application to identify any usability issues.

1. **Set Clear Objectives**: Define what you want to learn from the testing. Focus on specific tasks users should be able to complete.
2. **Recruit Participants**: Choose participants who represent your target audience. This will ensure that the feedback is relevant.
3. **Observe and Document**: Observe users as they perform tasks, noting

any difficulties or confusion they encounter.

7.2. Gathering Feedback

1. **Surveys and Questionnaires**: Use surveys to gather quantitative and qualitative feedback from users about their experience with the application.
2. **User Interviews**: Conduct interviews to gain deeper insights into user preferences, frustrations, and suggestions for improvement.
3. **Analytics Tools**: Implement analytics tools to track user behavior and interactions within the application. This data can help you identify areas for improvement.

7.3. Iterating on Design

Use the feedback gathered from testing and surveys to make informed design decisions. Regularly iterate on your UI/UX design based on user feedback to ensure continuous improvement.

Conclusion

In this chapter, we explored essential UI/UX design principles and how to implement them in your full-stack application. We covered topics such as responsive design, enhancing navigation and accessibility, leveraging Angular Material for UI components, best practices for form design, and the importance of user testing and feedback.

Chapter 9: Performance Optimization Techniques for Full-Stack Applications

Introduction

Performance optimization is a crucial aspect of web development that focuses on enhancing the speed and responsiveness of your application. Users expect web applications to load quickly and operate smoothly; slow applications can lead to frustration, abandonment, and a negative impact on user experience. In this chapter, we will explore various performance optimization techniques for your full-stack application built with ASP.NET Core and Angular.

We will cover the following topics:
1. Understanding Performance Metrics
2. Optimizing Backend Performance
3. Enhancing Frontend Performance
4. Efficient API Design and Implementation
5. Caching Strategies
6. Using Content Delivery Networks (CDNs)
7. Analyzing Performance with Tools

By the end of this chapter, you will have a comprehensive understanding of how to optimize the performance of your full-stack application effectively.

CHAPTER 9: PERFORMANCE OPTIMIZATION TECHNIQUES FOR...

1. Understanding Performance Metrics

Before diving into optimization techniques, it is essential to understand the various performance metrics that can help you evaluate your application's performance.

1.1. Key Performance Indicators (KPIs)

- **Page Load Time**: The time it takes for a page to fully load in a user's browser. Ideally, this should be under 2 seconds.
- **Time to First Byte (TTFB)**: The time it takes for the browser to receive the first byte of data from the server after making a request. A lower TTFB indicates better server performance.
- **First Contentful Paint (FCP)**: The time it takes for the browser to render the first piece of content (text or image) after the page starts loading. This metric reflects perceived load speed.
- **Time to Interactive (TTI)**: The time it takes for the page to become fully interactive, allowing users to click buttons and fill out forms.
- **Speed Index**: A metric that measures how quickly the contents of a page are visibly populated. A lower speed index indicates better performance.

1.2. Measuring Performance

To measure these performance metrics, you can use various tools, including:

- **Google PageSpeed Insights**: Analyzes the content of a web page and generates suggestions to make that page faster.
- **Lighthouse**: An open-source, automated tool for improving the quality of web pages. It runs audits for performance, accessibility, and more.
- **WebPageTest**: A tool that allows you to test your website's performance from multiple locations and on different browsers.

2. Optimizing Backend Performance

The backend of your application, built with ASP.NET Core, plays a significant role in overall performance. Here are some techniques to optimize backend performance:

2.1. Database Optimization

1. **Indexing**: Use indexes to speed up data retrieval operations. Identify frequently queried columns and create indexes on them to enhance performance.

```sql
Copy code
CREATE INDEX idx_product_name ON Products(Name);
```

1. **Query Optimization**: Analyze and optimize your database queries. Use tools like SQL Server Profiler to identify slow queries and optimize them by avoiding unnecessary joins and selecting only required columns.
2. **Connection Pooling**: Enable connection pooling to reduce the overhead of establishing a connection to the database. This allows your application to reuse existing connections instead of creating new ones for each request.
3. **Database Migrations**: Keep your database schema up to date using Entity Framework Core migrations. Regularly check for unnecessary tables or columns and clean them up.

2.2. Asynchronous Programming

Use asynchronous programming to improve the responsiveness of your application. By using async and await, you can prevent blocking the main thread while waiting for I/O operations to complete.

Example of an asynchronous controller action:

```csharp
Copy code
[HttpGet]
public async Task<ActionResult<Product>> GetProduct(int id)
{
    var product = await _context.Products.FindAsync(id);
    if (product == null)
    {
        return NotFound();
    }
    return product;
}
```

2.3. Minimize Middleware and Use Lightweight Services

While middleware is essential for handling requests, excessive or unnecessary middleware can slow down your application. Review the middleware you have configured and eliminate any that are not needed.

Additionally, use lightweight services where possible. For example, avoid large frameworks for simple tasks.

3. Enhancing Frontend Performance

Optimizing the frontend, built with Angular, is equally important for delivering a smooth user experience. Here are several strategies to enhance frontend performance:

3.1. Lazy Loading Modules

Implement lazy loading to load Angular modules only when they are needed. This technique reduces the initial load time of the application by splitting the application into smaller bundles.

1. **Setting Up Lazy Loading**: Update your routing configuration to use lazy loading:

```typescript
Copy code
const routes: Routes = [
  {
    path: 'products',
    loadChildren: () => import('./product/product.module').then(m
    => m.ProductModule)
  },
  {
    path: 'categories',
    loadChildren: () =>
    import('./category/category.module').then(m =>
    m.CategoryModule)
  }
];
```

3.2. Optimize Angular Bundle Size

1. **Tree Shaking**: Ensure that Angular's tree shaking feature is enabled. This eliminates unused code from the final bundle.
2. **AOT Compilation**: Use Ahead-of-Time (AOT) compilation to pre-compile your Angular templates during the build process. This reduces the size of the application and improves load times.

```bash
Copy code
ng build --prod --aot
```

1. **Minification and Uglification**: Enable minification during the build process to reduce the size of JavaScript and CSS files.

3.3. Use Change Detection Strategies Wisely

Angular's change detection can impact performance. Use OnPush change detection strategy for components that do not frequently change.

CHAPTER 9: PERFORMANCE OPTIMIZATION TECHNIQUES FOR...

```typescript
Copy code
@Component({
  selector: 'app-product',
  changeDetection: ChangeDetectionStrategy.OnPush,
  templateUrl: './product.component.html',
})
export class ProductComponent {
  // Component logic...
}
```

This tells Angular to check for changes only when input properties change or an event occurs within the component.

3.4. Optimize Images and Assets

1. **Image Formats**: Use appropriate image formats (e.g., WebP) and compress images to reduce file sizes.
2. **Responsive Images**: Use the <picture> element and srcset attribute to provide different image sizes for various screen resolutions.

```html
Copy code
<picture>
   <source srcset="image-small.webp" media="(max-width: 600px)">
   <img src="image-large.webp" alt="Description">
</picture>
```

1. **Cache Static Assets**: Configure HTTP caching for static assets to improve load times for returning users.

4. Efficient API Design and Implementation

Designing efficient APIs is crucial for ensuring that your frontend can retrieve data quickly and effectively. Here are some strategies for optimizing your API:

4.1. RESTful API Principles

1. **Use Appropriate HTTP Methods**: Follow RESTful principles by using the appropriate HTTP methods (GET, POST, PUT, DELETE) for your API endpoints.
2. **Versioning**: Implement API versioning to manage changes without disrupting existing clients. You can use URL versioning (e.g., /api/v1/products) or header versioning.

4.2. Limit Data Returned

Use filtering, sorting, and pagination to limit the amount of data returned by your API. This reduces the payload size and improves performance.

1. **Filtering**: Allow clients to specify query parameters to filter results.

```
csharp
Copy code
[HttpGet]
public async Task<ActionResult<IEnumerable<Product>>> GetProducts([FromQuery] string category = null)
{
    var query = _context.Products.AsQueryable();
    if (!string.IsNullOrEmpty(category))
    {
        query = query.Where(p => p.Category.Name == category);
    }
    return await query.ToListAsync();
}
```

1. **Pagination**: Implement pagination to return only a subset of results.

```csharp
Copy code
[HttpGet]
public async Task<ActionResult<IEnumerable<Product>>>
GetProducts(int page = 1, int pageSize = 10)
{
    return await _context.Products
        .Skip((page - 1) * pageSize)
        .Take(pageSize)
        .ToListAsync();
}
```

4.3. Optimize Database Queries

1. **Use Eager Loading**: Use eager loading to reduce the number of database calls when retrieving related data.

```csharp
Copy code
var products = await _context.Products
    .Include(p => p.Category)
    .ToListAsync();
```

1. **Avoid N+1 Queries**: Use proper relationships and loading strategies to avoid the N+1 query problem, where a query to fetch items results in additional queries for each item's related data.

5. Caching Strategies

Caching is a powerful technique for improving application performance by storing frequently accessed data in memory. This reduces the need for repeated database queries and API calls.

5.1. In-Memory Caching

ASP.NET Core provides built-in support for in-memory caching. You can cache data within the application to avoid repeated processing.

1. **Add Caching Services**: In Startup.cs, add caching services:

```csharp
Copy code
public void ConfigureServices(IServiceCollection services)
{
    services.AddMemoryCache();
    // Other services...
}
```

1. **Use Caching in Controllers**: Use the IMemoryCache interface to cache data in your controllers:

```csharp
Copy code
private readonly IMemoryCache _cache;

public ProductsController(ApplicationDbContext context, IMemoryCache cache)
{
    _context = context;
    _cache = cache;
}
```

CHAPTER 9: PERFORMANCE OPTIMIZATION TECHNIQUES FOR...

```
[HttpGet]
public async Task<ActionResult<IEnumerable<Product>>> GetProducts()
{
    if (!_cache.TryGetValue("products", out List<Product>
    products))
    {
        products = await _context.Products.ToListAsync();
        _cache.Set("products", products, TimeSpan.FromMinutes(5));
        // Cache for 5 minutes
    }
    return products;
}
```

5.2. Distributed Caching

For larger applications or those running in a distributed environment, consider using distributed caching solutions like Redis or SQL Server caching.

1. **Install Redis**: If you choose Redis, install the necessary NuGet package:

```bash
Copy code
Install-Package Microsoft.Extensions.Caching.StackExchangeRedis
```

1. **Configure Redis in Startup.cs**: In Startup.cs, configure Redis caching:

```csharp
Copy code
public void ConfigureServices(IServiceCollection services)
{
    services.AddStackExchangeRedisCache(options =>
    {
```

```
    options.Configuration = "localhost:6379"; // Redis server
    configuration
});
// Other services...
}
```

1. **Use Redis in Controllers**: Similar to in-memory caching, use IDistributedCache for distributed cache implementations.

```csharp
Copy code
private readonly IDistributedCache _cache;

public ProductsController(ApplicationDbContext context,
IDistributedCache cache)
{
    _context = context;
    _cache = cache;
}

[HttpGet]
public async Task<ActionResult<IEnumerable<Product>>> GetProducts()
{
    var cacheKey = "products";
    var cachedProducts = await _cache.GetStringAsync(cacheKey);

    if (cachedProducts != null)
    {
        return
        JsonConvert.DeserializeObject<List<Product>>(cachedProducts);
    }

    var products = await _context.Products.ToListAsync();
    await _cache.SetStringAsync(cacheKey,
    JsonConvert.SerializeObject(products), new
```

```
    DistributedCacheEntryOptions
    {
        AbsoluteExpirationRelativeToNow = TimeSpan.FromMinutes(5)
    });

    return products;
}
```

5.3. HTTP Caching

Implement HTTP caching to cache responses at the browser or intermediary proxies. You can control cache behavior using HTTP headers.

1. **Cache-Control Header**: Use the Cache-Control header in your API responses to specify caching policies.

```csharp
Copy code
[HttpGet]
[ResponseCache(Duration = 60)] // Cache for 60 seconds
public async Task<ActionResult<IEnumerable<Product>>> GetProducts()
{
    return await _context.Products.ToListAsync();
}
```

6. Using Content Delivery Networks (CDNs)

A Content Delivery Network (CDN) is a network of distributed servers that deliver content to users based on their geographic location. Using a CDN can significantly improve the performance of your application, especially for static assets such as images, stylesheets, and scripts.

6.1. Setting Up a CDN

1. **Choose a CDN Provider**: Select a CDN provider that suits your needs.

Popular options include Cloudflare, AWS CloudFront, and Akamai.
2. **Configure Your Assets**: Upload your static assets (e.g., images, CSS, JavaScript) to the CDN. Most providers offer easy integration with your existing application.
3. **Update Asset URLs**: Update your application to use the CDN URLs for static assets. For example:

```
html
Copy code
<link rel="stylesheet" href="https://cdn.example.com/styles.css">
<script src="https://cdn.example.com/scripts.js"></script>
<img src="https://cdn.example.com/images/logo.png" alt="Logo">
```

6.2. Benefits of Using a CDN

- **Reduced Latency**: CDNs deliver content from servers closer to the user, reducing latency and improving load times.
- **Load Balancing**: Distributes traffic across multiple servers, improving scalability and performance during peak usage.
- **DDoS Protection**: Many CDNs offer security features to protect against Distributed Denial of Service (DDoS) attacks.

7. Analyzing Performance with Tools

To effectively optimize performance, you need to analyze your application regularly. Various tools can help you identify bottlenecks and areas for improvement.

7.1. Profiling Tools

1. **ASP.NET Core Application Insights**: This tool provides real-time monitoring and performance analytics for your ASP.NET Core applications. It helps you identify performance bottlenecks, track request rates, and analyze failures.

- **Setup**: Add the Application Insights SDK to your project and configure it in Startup.cs.

1. **DotTrace**: JetBrains DotTrace is a powerful profiling tool for .NET applications. It allows you to analyze CPU and memory usage and identify performance issues in your code.
2. **Browser Developer Tools**: Use built-in developer tools in browsers (e.g., Chrome, Firefox) to analyze network requests, inspect resource loading times, and view performance metrics like FCP and TTI.

7.2. Load Testing Tools

1. **Apache JMeter**: An open-source load testing tool that allows you to simulate multiple users and analyze application performance under stress.
2. **k6**: A modern load testing tool that provides a scripting API to simulate user interactions. It's particularly useful for testing APIs and microservices.
3. **Gatling**: A powerful load testing framework for web applications that helps you analyze performance under varying loads.

Conclusion

In this chapter, we explored various performance optimization techniques for your full-stack application using ASP.NET Core and Angular. We discussed the importance of understanding performance metrics, optimizing backend and frontend performance, designing efficient APIs, implementing caching strategies, leveraging CDNs, and analyzing performance with various tools.

Chapter 10: Deploying Your Full-Stack Application

Introduction

Deployment is a crucial step in the software development lifecycle that involves making your application available for users. Deploying a full-stack application can be complex, especially when you have different technologies for the frontend and backend, as in the case of ASP.NET Core and Angular. In this chapter, we will explore various deployment strategies, best practices, and tools that can help you successfully deploy your full-stack application.

We will cover the following topics:
1. Preparing Your Application for Deployment
2. Hosting Options for ASP.NET Core
3. Hosting Options for Angular
4. Continuous Integration and Continuous Deployment (CI/CD)
5. Configuring a Production Environment
6. Monitoring and Logging in Production
7. Post-Deployment Best Practices

By the end of this chapter, you will have a solid understanding of how to deploy your full-stack application effectively and maintain it in a production environment.

1. Preparing Your Application for Deployment

Before deploying your application, it's essential to ensure that it is production-ready. This involves a series of steps to optimize performance, secure sensitive information, and remove any unnecessary code.

1.1. Build and Optimize Your Application

1. **Build for Production**: For both ASP.NET Core and Angular, you should build your application in production mode to optimize performance.

    - For **ASP.NET Core**, publish your application:

```bash
Copy code
dotnet publish -c Release
```

   1. This command compiles your application and copies the necessary files to the bin/Release/net5.0/publish directory.

    - For **Angular**, build your application with the production flag:

```bash
Copy code
ng build --prod
```

   1. This command creates a production-ready version of your Angular

application in the dist/ folder.
2. **Remove Unused Code**: Ensure that you remove any unused components, services, and libraries from your codebase. This will reduce the overall size of your application and minimize security risks.

1.2. Environment Configuration

Different environments (development, testing, production) may require different configuration settings. Use environment-specific configuration files for your ASP.NET Core application.

1. **appsettings.json**: Create separate configuration files for different environments, such as appsettings.Development.json and appsettings.Production.json.
2. Example structure:

```json
Copy code
{
  "ConnectionStrings": {
    "DefaultConnection": "Server=your_server;Database=YourDatabase;Trusted_Connection=True;"
  },
  "Jwt": {
    "Key": "Your_Production_Secret_Key",
    "Issuer": "YourApp",
    "Audience": "YourAppUsers"
  }
}
```

1. **Use Environment Variables**: Use environment variables for sensitive information like database connection strings and API keys. This helps keep sensitive data out of your source code.

CHAPTER 10: DEPLOYING YOUR FULL-STACK APPLICATION

2. Hosting Options for ASP.NET Core

When it comes to hosting your ASP.NET Core application, you have several options to choose from. Each hosting environment has its advantages and disadvantages.

2.1. Self-Hosting

ASP.NET Core applications can be self-hosted using Kestrel, which is the default web server included with ASP.NET Core. This is a good option for development or small-scale applications.

1. **Run Kestrel Locally**: You can run your application using Kestrel by executing the following command:

```bash
Copy code
dotnet run
```

1. **Production Considerations**: While self-hosting can be convenient, it is generally recommended to use a reverse proxy server (like Nginx or Apache) in a production environment for better performance and security.

2.2. Cloud Hosting

1. **Microsoft Azure**: Azure App Service is a popular option for hosting ASP.NET Core applications. It offers a fully managed platform with automatic scaling, continuous deployment, and integrated monitoring.

   - **Deploying to Azure**: You can publish your application directly from Visual Studio or use Azure CLI commands.

1. **AWS Elastic Beanstalk**: AWS Elastic Beanstalk is another excellent option for hosting ASP.NET Core applications. It provides a quick and easy way to deploy and manage applications in the AWS cloud.

- **Deploying to Elastic Beanstalk**: You can use the AWS Toolkit for Visual Studio to publish your application directly.

1. **DigitalOcean and Heroku**: Both DigitalOcean and Heroku provide platforms for deploying web applications with minimal setup. They offer different levels of management and scaling options.

3. Hosting Options for Angular

Angular applications are typically served as static files, making them easy to host on various platforms. Here are some popular hosting options for Angular:

3.1. Static File Hosting

1. **GitHub Pages**: GitHub Pages is a simple way to host your Angular application for free. You can publish your application by pushing it to a GitHub repository.
2. **Netlify**: Netlify offers free hosting for static websites and provides features like continuous deployment from GitHub and built-in HTTPS.
3. **Vercel**: Vercel is another excellent option for hosting Angular applications. It provides fast deployments and a user-friendly interface.

3.2. Cloud Hosting

1. **Firebase Hosting**: Firebase Hosting is a fast and secure way to host your Angular application. It provides a simple command-line interface for deployment.

- **Deploying to Firebase**: Install the Firebase CLI and initialize your

CHAPTER 10: DEPLOYING YOUR FULL-STACK APPLICATION

project:

```bash
Copy code
npm install -g firebase-tools
firebase init
firebase deploy
```

1. **AWS S3 and CloudFront**: You can host your Angular application on Amazon S3 and use CloudFront as a CDN to deliver content quickly.

- **Deploying to S3**: Build your Angular application and upload the contents of the dist/ folder to your S3 bucket.

4. Continuous Integration and Continuous Deployment (CI/CD)

Implementing CI/CD pipelines can greatly enhance your deployment process by automating builds, tests, and deployments. This helps ensure that your application is always in a deployable state.

4.1. Setting Up CI/CD Pipelines

1. **Choose a CI/CD Tool**: Popular CI/CD tools include Jenkins, GitHub Actions, GitLab CI/CD, and CircleCI. Each tool has its unique features and integrations.
2. **Create a CI/CD Pipeline**: A typical CI/CD pipeline includes stages for:

- **Build**: Compile the application and run tests.
- **Test**: Execute automated tests to verify the application's functionality.
- **Deploy**: Deploy the application to the desired environment.

1. **Example GitHub Actions Workflow**: Here's an example of a GitHub Actions workflow for deploying an Angular application:

```yaml
Copy code
name: Deploy Angular App

on:
  push:
    branches:
      - main

jobs:
  build:
    runs-on: ubuntu-latest

    steps:
    - name: Checkout Code
      uses: actions/checkout@v2

    - name: Install Dependencies
      run: npm install

    - name: Build Application
      run: npm run build --prod

    - name: Deploy to Firebase
      run: npm install -g firebase-tools
      run: firebase deploy --token ${{ secrets.FIREBASE_TOKEN }}
```

This workflow builds the Angular application and deploys it to Firebase when code is pushed to the main branch.

4.2. Setting Up Automated Testing

Integrate automated testing in your CI/CD pipeline to ensure that any changes do not break existing functionality. Use testing frameworks like Jasmine and Protractor for Angular, and xUnit or NUnit for ASP.NET Core.

5. Configuring a Production Environment

Configuring a production environment is essential for ensuring the reliability and security of your application. Here are some key considerations:

5.1. Environment Variables

Use environment variables to manage configuration settings specific to your production environment. This includes sensitive information like database connection strings and API keys.

1. **Setting Environment Variables**: On your hosting platform, set the necessary environment variables. For example, in Azure, you can set application settings in the Azure portal.

5.2. Security Configuration

1. **HTTPS**: Ensure that your application is served over HTTPS to encrypt data in transit. Configure your web server (e.g., Nginx, Apache) to enforce HTTPS.
2. **Authentication and Authorization**: Make sure authentication and authorization are correctly configured, and sensitive endpoints are protected.
3. **CORS Policies**: Configure Cross-Origin Resource Sharing (CORS) policies to allow only trusted domains to access your API.

```csharp
Copy code
services.AddCors(options =>
{
    options.AddPolicy("AllowSpecificOrigin",
        builder =>
        builder.WithOrigins("https://your-frontend-domain.com")
               .AllowAnyHeader()
               .AllowAnyMethod());
```

```
});
```

5.3. Logging and Monitoring

Implement logging and monitoring to track application performance and identify issues in real time.

1. **Logging**: Use logging frameworks like Serilog or NLog to log important events and errors.
2. **Monitoring Tools**: Use tools like Application Insights or New Relic to monitor application performance and receive alerts for potential issues.

6. Monitoring and Logging in Production

Monitoring and logging are critical for maintaining the health of your application in a production environment. They allow you to track performance, diagnose issues, and ensure that your application runs smoothly.

6.1. Implementing Application Insights

1. **Integrate Application Insights**: To integrate Application Insights into your ASP.NET Core application, install the necessary NuGet package:

```bash
Copy code
Install-Package Microsoft.ApplicationInsights.AspNetCore
```

1. **Configure Application Insights**: In your Startup.cs, configure Application Insights:

```csharp
Copy code
public void ConfigureServices
(IServiceCollection services)
{
    services.AddApplicationInsightsTelemetry
(Configuration["ApplicationInsights:
InstrumentationKey"]);
}
```

1. **Track Custom Events**: Use the Application Insights SDK to track custom events and metrics:

```csharp
Copy code
private readonly TelemetryClient _telemetryClient;

public ProductsController(TelemetryClient telemetryClient)
{
    _telemetryClient = telemetryClient;
}

[HttpGet]
public async Task<ActionResult<
Product>> GetProduct(int id)
{
    _telemetryClient.TrackEvent("GetProductCalled", new
    Dictionary<string, string>
    {
        { "ProductId", id.ToString() }
    });

    var product = await _context.Products.FindAsync(id);
    if (product == null)
    {
        _telemetryClient.TrackEvent("ProductNotFound", new
```

```
            Dictionary<string, string>
            {
                { "ProductId", id.ToString() }
            });
            return NotFound();
    }
    return product;
}
```

6.2. Centralized Logging

1. **Use Serilog for Centralized Logging**: Serilog is a popular logging library that supports structured logging and can send logs to various sinks (e.g., files, databases, cloud services).

- **Install Serilog**: Install the Serilog NuGet packages:

```bash
Copy code
Install-Package Serilog.AspNetCore
Install-Package Serilog.Sinks.File
```

- **Configure Serilog**: In your Program.cs, configure Serilog:

```csharp
Copy code
public class Program
{
    public static void Main(string[] args)
    {
        Log.Logger = new LoggerConfiguration()
            .MinimumLevel.Information()
            .WriteTo.File("logs/myapp.txt",
```

CHAPTER 10: DEPLOYING YOUR FULL-STACK APPLICATION

```
rollingInterval: RollingInterval.Day)
        .CreateLogger();

    try
    {
        Log.Information("Starting web host");
        CreateHostBuilder(args).Build().Run();
    }
    catch (Exception ex)
    {
        Log.Fatal(ex, "Application start-up failed");
    }
    finally
    {
        Log.CloseAndFlush();
    }
}

public static IHostBuilder
CreateHostBuilder(string[] args) =>
    Host.CreateDefaultBuilder(args)
        .UseSerilog() // Add this line
        .ConfigureWebHostDefaults(webBuilder =>
        {
            webBuilder.UseStartup<Startup>();
        });
}
```

1. **Log Events and Exceptions**: Use Serilog to log important events and exceptions throughout your application:

```
csharp
Copy code
[HttpPost]
public async Task<ActionResult<Product>>
CreateProduct(Product product)
```

```csharp
{
    try
    {
        _context.Products.Add(product);
        await _context.SaveChangesAsync();
        Log.Information("Product created: {ProductId}", product.Id);
        return CreatedAtAction
(nameof(GetProduct), new { id = product.Id }, product);
    }
    catch (Exception ex)
    {
        Log.Error(ex, "Error creating product");
        return StatusCode(500, "Internal server error");
    }
}
```

7. Post-Deployment Best Practices

Once your application is deployed, it's essential to follow best practices to maintain its performance and reliability.

7.1. Regular Updates and Maintenance

1. **Keep Dependencies Updated**: Regularly check for updates to your libraries and frameworks to ensure you have the latest security patches and features.
2. **Monitor Performance**: Continuously monitor the performance of your application using the tools discussed earlier. Set up alerts for any performance degradation or errors.

7.2. Backup and Recovery Plans

1. **Implement Regular Backups**: Set up automated backups for your database and application files to prevent data loss in case of failure.
2. **Test Recovery Procedures**: Regularly test your backup and recovery

procedures to ensure that you can restore your application quickly if necessary.

7.3. User Feedback and Iteration

1. **Collect User Feedback**: Regularly gather feedback from users to understand their experiences and areas for improvement.
2. **Iterate on Features**: Use user feedback to iterate on features and enhance the overall experience of your application.

Conclusion

In this chapter, we explored the essential steps and best practices for deploying your full-stack application. We discussed how to prepare your application for deployment, hosting options for both the ASP.NET Core backend and Angular frontend, and the importance of CI/CD for automating deployments.

We also covered how to configure a production environment, implement monitoring and logging, and follow post-deployment best practices to maintain your application's performance. By applying these techniques, you can ensure that your application runs smoothly in a production environment and continues to meet user needs effectively.

Chapter 11: Security Best Practices for Full-Stack Applications

Introduction

In today's digital landscape, security is paramount for web applications. With the increasing frequency and sophistication of cyberattacks, developers must prioritize securing their applications to protect user data and maintain trust. This chapter will explore essential security best practices for full-stack applications, specifically those built with ASP.NET Core for the backend and Angular for the frontend.

We will cover the following topics:
1. Understanding Security Fundamentals
2. Securing the ASP.NET Core Backend
3. Securing the Angular Frontend
4. Implementing Authentication and Authorization
5. Data Protection Strategies
6. Protecting Against Common Vulnerabilities
7. Security Testing and Monitoring

By the end of this chapter, you will have a comprehensive understanding of how to secure your full-stack application effectively.

CHAPTER 11: SECURITY BEST PRACTICES FOR FULL-STACK...

1. Understanding Security Fundamentals

1.1. The Importance of Security

Security is crucial for maintaining the confidentiality, integrity, and availability of data. A security breach can lead to:

- Data loss or theft
- Unauthorized access to sensitive information
- Damage to an organization's reputation
- Legal consequences and financial losses

1.2. Security Principles

1. **Least Privilege**: Grant users the minimum level of access necessary to perform their tasks. This minimizes the risk of unauthorized access to sensitive resources.
2. **Defense in Depth**: Implement multiple layers of security controls throughout your application to provide redundancy. If one layer fails, others will still provide protection.
3. **Fail Securely**: Ensure that when errors or failures occur, the system fails in a secure manner that does not expose sensitive data or create vulnerabilities.
4. **Regular Security Audits**: Conduct regular security assessments and audits to identify vulnerabilities and ensure compliance with security policies.

2. Securing the ASP.NET Core Backend

The ASP.NET Core backend is responsible for handling requests, processing data, and interacting with databases. Securing this layer is critical for protecting sensitive information.

2.1. Use HTTPS

Always serve your application over HTTPS to encrypt data in transit. This protects sensitive information from being intercepted by attackers.

1. **Enforcing HTTPS**: In Startup.cs, enforce HTTPS redirection:

```csharp
Copy code
public void Configure(IApplicationBuilder app, IWebHostEnvironment env)
{
    app.UseHttpsRedirection();
    // Other middleware...
}
```

1. **Obtain an SSL Certificate**: Obtain an SSL certificate from a trusted Certificate Authority (CA) to secure your application.
2. **2. Secure API Endpoints**
3. **Implement Authentication**: Use authentication mechanisms (such as JWT tokens) to secure your API endpoints and ensure that only authenticated users can access sensitive resources.
4. **Authorize Access**: Use role-based access control (RBAC) to restrict access to specific endpoints based on user roles.

```csharp
Copy code
[Authorize(Roles = "Admin")]
[HttpPost]
public async Task<ActionResult<Product>> CreateProduct(Product product)
{
    // Implementation...
}
```

1. **Use CORS Policies**: Configure Cross-Origin Resource Sharing (CORS)

CHAPTER 11: SECURITY BEST PRACTICES FOR FULL-STACK...

to restrict which domains can access your API.

```csharp
Copy code
services.AddCors(options =>
{
    options.AddPolicy("AllowSpecificOrigin",
        builder =>
        builder.WithOrigins("https://your-frontend-domain.com")
                       .AllowAnyHeader()
                       .AllowAnyMethod());
});
```

2.3. Input Validation and Sanitization

1. **Validate User Input**: Use data annotations to enforce validation rules on model properties, ensuring that only valid data is processed.
2. **Sanitize Inputs**: Sanitize any user inputs to prevent injection attacks, such as SQL injection or cross-site scripting (XSS).

```csharp
Copy code
[HttpPost]
public async Task<ActionResult<Product>> CreateProduct([FromBody] Product product)
{
    // Sanitize input...
    product.Name = WebUtility.HtmlEncode(product.Name);
    // Other validations...
}
```

3. Securing the Angular Frontend

The Angular frontend is responsible for presenting data to users and collecting their input. Securing this layer is equally important to prevent unauthorized access and data breaches.

3.1. Protecting Routes

1. **Use Route Guards**: Implement route guards to protect routes from unauthorized access. Use the Angular AuthGuard to ensure only authenticated users can access specific routes.

```typescript
Copy code
import { Injectable } from '@angular/core';
import { CanActivate, ActivatedRouteSnapshot, RouterStateSnapshot
} from '@angular/router';
import { AuthService } from './auth.service';

@Injectable({
  providedIn: 'root'
})
export class AuthGuard implements CanActivate {
  constructor(private authService: AuthService) {}

  canActivate(
    next: ActivatedRouteSnapshot,
    state: RouterStateSnapshot): boolean {
    return this.authService.isLoggedIn();
  }
}
```

3.2. Avoiding XSS Vulnerabilities

1. **Use Angular's Built-in Sanitization**: Angular automatically sanitizes user input to prevent XSS attacks. Use Angular's built-in mechanisms (e.g., [innerHTML] binding) carefully.

```html
html
Copy code
<div [innerHTML]="sanitizedHtml"></div>
```

1. **Escape User Input**: Always escape any user-generated content before rendering it to prevent XSS attacks.

3.3. Securing API Calls

1. **Use HTTPS for API Calls**: Ensure that all API calls are made over HTTPS to encrypt data in transit.
2. **Implement Token Expiry and Refresh**: Implement token expiration and refresh mechanisms to enhance security. Expired tokens should require the user to re-authenticate.

```typescript
typescript
Copy code
const tokenExpiryTime = 3600; // 1 hour
setTimeout(() => {
  this.authService.refreshToken();
}, tokenExpiryTime * 1000);
```

4. Implementing Authentication and Authorization

Effective authentication and authorization are fundamental for securing your application. Implement these mechanisms to control access to sensitive resources.

4.1. Authentication Strategies

1. **JWT Authentication**: Use JSON Web Tokens (JWT) for stateless

authentication. Upon successful login, generate a JWT token and send it back to the client.
2. **OAuth2 and OpenID Connect**: Consider implementing OAuth2 or OpenID Connect for authentication. These protocols allow users to authenticate using third-party providers (e.g., Google, Facebook).

4.2. Authorization Strategies

1. **Role-Based Access Control (RBAC)**: Implement RBAC to restrict access based on user roles. Ensure that sensitive operations are only accessible to users with the appropriate roles.
2. **Claims-Based Authorization**: Use claims-based authorization to define fine-grained access control based on user attributes.

5. Data Protection Strategies

Protecting sensitive data is essential to prevent data breaches and unauthorized access. Implement these strategies to safeguard user data.

5.1. Encrypt Sensitive Data

1. **Database Encryption**: Use database encryption to protect sensitive data stored in your database. This ensures that even if the database is compromised, the data remains secure.
2. **File Encryption**: If your application stores sensitive files (e.g., user-uploaded documents), ensure they are encrypted before being saved.

5.2. Secure Configuration Settings

1. **Use Configuration Providers**: Use ASP.NET Core's configuration providers to manage sensitive information through environment variables, user secrets, or Azure Key Vault.

```csharp
Copy code
public void ConfigureServices(IServiceCollection services)
{
    var keyVaultEndpoint = new
    Uri(Configuration["KeyVault:Endpoint"]);
    var client = new SecretClient(keyVaultEndpoint, new
    DefaultAzureCredential());
    services.AddAzureKeyVault(client);
}
```

1. **Avoid Hardcoding Secrets**: Never hardcode sensitive information (like API keys or connection strings) in your source code. Use configuration files or environment variables instead.

6. Protecting Against Common Vulnerabilities

Understanding common vulnerabilities is essential for building secure applications. Here are some of the most prevalent security threats and how to mitigate them:

6.1. SQL Injection

SQL Injection occurs when an attacker injects malicious SQL code into an input field, potentially compromising the database.

1. **Use Parameterized Queries**: Always use parameterized queries or prepared statements to prevent SQL injection.

```csharp
Copy code
var products = await _context.Products
    .FromSqlRaw("SELECT * FROM Products WHERE Name = {0}",
    productName)
```

```
.ToListAsync();
```

6.2. Cross-Site Scripting (XSS)

XSS attacks occur when an attacker injects malicious scripts into web pages viewed by other users.

1. **Sanitize User Input**: Sanitize any user-generated content before displaying it on the page.
2. **Use CSP (Content Security Policy)**: Implement a Content Security Policy to control which resources can be loaded and executed in your application.

6.3. Cross-Site Request Forgery (CSRF)

CSRF attacks occur when a malicious site tricks a user into submitting a request without their consent.

1. **Use Anti-CSRF Tokens**: Implement anti-CSRF tokens in forms to validate requests.

```csharp
Copy code
services.AddAntiforgery(options => options.HeaderName = "X-CSRF-TOKEN");
```

Chapter 12: Continuous Improvement and Future Enhancements

Introduction

As the technology landscape continues to evolve, so do user expectations and security threats. Continuous improvement is essential for maintaining the relevance, performance, and security of your full-stack application built with ASP.NET Core and Angular. This chapter will delve into strategies for fostering continuous improvement and planning future enhancements to ensure your application meets the changing needs of users and stays ahead of emerging threats.

We will cover the following topics:
1. Establishing a Culture of Continuous Improvement
2. Incorporating User Feedback
3. Staying Updated with Technology Trends
4. Planning for Scalability
5. Enhancing Security Posture
6. Leveraging Analytics for Decision-Making
7. Preparing for New Features and Upgrades

By the end of this chapter, you will have a comprehensive understanding of how to sustain and enhance your application over time.

1. Establishing a Culture of Continuous Improvement

Continuous improvement involves regularly assessing and enhancing your application to optimize performance, user experience, and security. Creating a culture of continuous improvement within your development team is essential for the long-term success of your application.

1.1. Encourage Open Communication

Foster an environment where team members feel comfortable sharing ideas, feedback, and concerns. Encourage regular discussions on areas for improvement and invite team members to contribute to the decision-making process.

1.2. Implement Agile Practices

Adopt Agile methodologies, such as Scrum or Kanban, to facilitate iterative development and continuous feedback. Agile practices enable teams to respond quickly to changes and improve the application incrementally.

1.3. Conduct Regular Retrospectives

Schedule regular retrospectives to review what went well, what didn't, and how the team can improve. This practice helps identify opportunities for growth and encourages a mindset of continuous learning.

1.4. Foster a Learning Environment

Encourage team members to pursue professional development opportunities, such as attending conferences, participating in workshops, or completing online courses. This commitment to learning will help your team stay updated with industry best practices and emerging technologies.

2. Incorporating User Feedback

User feedback is a valuable source of information that can guide the continuous improvement of your application. Actively seeking and incorporating user feedback can help you identify pain points and prioritize enhancements.

2.1. User Surveys and Questionnaires

Conduct regular surveys and questionnaires to gather feedback from users about their experiences with your application. Use targeted questions to

CHAPTER 12: CONTINUOUS IMPROVEMENT AND FUTURE ENHANCEMENTS

understand their needs, preferences, and any challenges they face.

1. **Example Questions**:

- What features do you find most valuable?
- Are there any features that you find confusing or difficult to use?
- How would you rate the performance of the application?
- What additional features would you like to see?

2.2. User Interviews

Conduct one-on-one interviews with users to gain deeper insights into their experiences. This qualitative approach allows you to ask follow-up questions and clarify responses.

2.3. Usability Testing

Regularly conduct usability testing to observe how users interact with your application. Identify any areas of confusion or difficulty, and gather feedback on potential improvements.

1. **Test Scenarios**:

- Ask users to complete specific tasks (e.g., creating an account, making a purchase).
- Observe their interactions and note any challenges they encounter.

2.4. Feedback Mechanisms within the Application

Implement feedback mechanisms directly within the application, such as a feedback form or a "Report an Issue" button. This allows users to provide feedback in real time and report any problems they encounter.

3. Staying Updated with Technology Trends

The technology landscape is constantly changing, with new frameworks, libraries, and tools emerging regularly. Staying updated with these trends is crucial for maintaining a competitive edge and ensuring your application remains relevant.

3.1. Follow Industry News and Blogs

Subscribe to industry news sources, blogs, and newsletters to stay informed about the latest developments in web technologies and best practices.

1. **Recommended Sources**:

- Smashing Magazine
- Dev.to
- Medium
- TechCrunch

3.2. Participate in Online Communities

Engage with online communities and forums, such as Stack Overflow, Reddit, and GitHub. Participate in discussions, ask questions, and share your knowledge with others.

3.3. Attend Conferences and Meetups

Attend industry conferences, meetups, and webinars to learn from experts, network with peers, and gain insights into emerging trends and technologies.

3.4. Experiment with New Technologies

Encourage your team to experiment with new technologies and frameworks in small projects or prototypes. This hands-on experience will help you evaluate whether new tools could benefit your application.

CHAPTER 12: CONTINUOUS IMPROVEMENT AND FUTURE ENHANCEMENTS

4. Planning for Scalability

As your user base grows, your application must be able to scale effectively to accommodate increased demand. Proper planning for scalability ensures that your application can handle future growth without sacrificing performance.

4.1. Horizontal and Vertical Scaling

1. **Horizontal Scaling**: Involves adding more instances of your application (e.g., multiple servers) to distribute the load. This approach allows for greater flexibility and redundancy.
2. **Vertical Scaling**: Involves upgrading the existing server (e.g., adding more CPU, RAM, or storage). While this can be simpler, it has limitations, as there is a maximum capacity for any single server.

4.2. Use Load Balancers

Implement load balancers to distribute incoming traffic across multiple server instances. Load balancing helps ensure that no single server is overwhelmed and enhances application reliability.

4.3. Optimize Database Performance

1. **Database Sharding**: Divide your database into smaller, more manageable pieces (shards) to improve performance and scalability.
2. **Replication**: Use database replication to create copies of your database for read operations. This can reduce the load on your primary database and improve performance.

4.4. Implement Microservices Architecture

Consider adopting a microservices architecture to enable independent scaling of different application components. This approach allows you to scale only the parts of your application that require it, rather than the entire application.

5. Enhancing Security Posture

As new threats emerge, it is vital to continuously improve your application's security posture. Regularly reviewing and enhancing your security measures will help protect user data and maintain trust.

5.1. Conduct Security Audits

Regularly conduct security audits to identify vulnerabilities and assess the effectiveness of your security measures. Engage third-party security experts to perform penetration testing and code reviews.

5.2. Stay Informed About Security Threats

Stay informed about the latest security threats and vulnerabilities that could impact your application. Subscribe to security mailing lists and follow security experts on social media.

1. **Resources**:

   - OWASP (Open Web Application Security Project)
   - CVE (Common Vulnerabilities and Exposures)
   - NIST (National Institute of Standards and Technology)

5.3. Regularly Update Dependencies

Regularly update your application's dependencies to ensure that you are using the latest versions with security patches. Use tools like npm audit for Node.js projects or NuGet Package Manager for ASP.NET Core projects to identify outdated or vulnerable packages.

5.4. Implement Security Headers

Use HTTP security headers to protect your application from common attacks, such as XSS, clickjacking, and content type sniffing. Configure the following headers in your ASP.NET Core application:

1. **Content Security Policy (CSP)**: Helps prevent XSS attacks by specifying which sources of content are trusted.

```csharp
Copy code
app.UseCsp(options => options
    .BlockAllMixedContent()
    .DefaultSources(s => s.Self())
    .ScriptSources(s =>
    s.Self().CustomSources("https://trusted-source.com"))
);
```

1. **X-Frame-Options**: Prevents clickjacking attacks by controlling whether your content can be embedded in frames.

```csharp
Copy code
app.UseXFrameOptions(options => options.SameOrigin());
```

1. **X-XSS-Protection**: Enables the XSS filter built into browsers.

```csharp
Copy code
app.UseXssProtection(options => options.Enabled());
```

6. Leveraging Analytics for Decision-Making

Data analytics can provide valuable insights into user behavior, application performance, and areas for improvement. Leveraging analytics can inform your decision-making processes and drive continuous improvement.

6.1. Implementing User Analytics

1. **Use Google Analytics**: Integrate Google Analytics into your Angular application to track user interactions, page views, and session duration.

```typescript
Copy code
import { Injectable } from '@angular/core';
import { Router, NavigationEnd } from '@angular/router';
import { filter } from 'rxjs/operators';

@Injectable({
  providedIn: 'root',
})
export class AnalyticsService {
  constructor(private router: Router) {
    this.router.events
      .pipe(filter(event => event instanceof NavigationEnd))
      .subscribe(() => {
        // Track page views
        gtag('config', 'GA_MEASUREMENT_ID', {
          page_path: this.router.url,
        });
      });
  }
}
```

1. **Analyze User Behavior**: Use analytics data to identify popular features, user drop-off points, and areas where users encounter difficulties. This information can guide future enhancements and optimizations.

6.2. Performance Monitoring

1. **Real User Monitoring (RUM)**: Implement RUM tools to gather performance data from real users. This data can help you understand how your application performs in the wild and identify areas for improvement.

CHAPTER 12: CONTINUOUS IMPROVEMENT AND FUTURE ENHANCEMENTS

2. **Synthetic Monitoring**: Use synthetic monitoring tools to simulate user interactions and measure application performance under various conditions.

7. Preparing for New Features and Upgrades

As your application evolves, you will likely want to add new features and make upgrades to improve functionality. Planning for these changes is essential to minimize disruptions and maintain application stability.

7.1. Prioritize Features Based on User Feedback

Use the feedback gathered from users to prioritize new features. Focus on enhancements that align with user needs and have the potential to provide the most significant impact.

1. **Feature Roadmap**: Create a roadmap that outlines planned features and enhancements, including timelines and resource allocation.

7.2. Implement Feature Flags

Feature flags allow you to deploy new features incrementally without exposing them to all users at once. This approach helps you test new features in production and gather feedback before a full rollout.

1. **Using Feature Flags**: Implement feature flags in your application to control which features are visible to users.

```csharp
Copy code
public class FeatureFlags
{
    public bool NewFeatureEnabled { get; set; }
}
```

1. **Configuring Feature Flags**: Store feature flag configurations in your appsettings.json or an external configuration service.

7.3. Regularly Plan Upgrades

Regularly assess the need for upgrades to your application's frameworks and libraries. Upgrading can provide performance improvements, new features, and security patches.

1. **Create an Upgrade Schedule**: Develop a schedule for regularly reviewing and upgrading dependencies, including Angular, ASP.NET Core, and third-party libraries.
2. **Testing Before Upgrades**: Before implementing upgrades, thoroughly test your application to identify any potential compatibility issues.

Conclusion

In this chapter, we explored the essential strategies for continuous improvement and future enhancements of your full-stack application. We discussed the importance of establishing a culture of continuous improvement, incorporating user feedback, staying updated with technology trends, and planning for scalability.

We also covered enhancing security posture, leveraging analytics for decision-making, and preparing for new features and upgrades. By applying these strategies, you can ensure that your application remains relevant, secure, and capable of meeting the evolving needs of your users.

Chapter 13: Community and Support in Application Development

Introduction

The development and success of any application extend beyond coding and deployment. Building a strong community around your application, fostering user engagement, and providing ongoing support are crucial for its longevity and relevance. In this chapter, we will explore the importance of community and support in application development, focusing on strategies for engaging users, encouraging collaboration, and leveraging feedback for continuous improvement.

We will cover the following topics:
1. Understanding the Value of Community
2. Building an Engaged User Community
3. Encouraging User Feedback and Contributions
4. Creating Support Channels
5. Leveraging Open Source Development
6. Utilizing Social Media and Online Platforms
7. Maintaining a Positive Community Environment

By the end of this chapter, you will have a solid understanding of how to cultivate a supportive community for your application and utilize that community to drive growth and improvement.

1. Understanding the Value of Community

1.1. What Is Community in Application Development?

In the context of application development, a community consists of users, developers, and contributors who interact around the application. This can include:

- **End Users**: Individuals who use your application to achieve specific goals or solve problems.
- **Developers**: Individuals who contribute to the application's codebase, whether through open-source contributions or internal development teams.
- **Support Personnel**: Individuals responsible for providing assistance and resolving issues for users.

1.2. The Benefits of Building a Community

1. **User Loyalty and Retention**: A strong community fosters user loyalty. When users feel connected to the application and its development process, they are more likely to continue using it and advocate for it within their networks.
2. **Continuous Feedback**: Engaging with your community allows you to gather valuable feedback that can guide future development and improvements. Users can provide insights into their needs and preferences, helping you prioritize features and enhancements.
3. **Knowledge Sharing**: A community encourages knowledge sharing among users and developers. This can lead to innovative ideas, solutions to common challenges, and improved practices.
4. **Support Network**: An engaged community can serve as a support network, providing users with resources and assistance. This reduces

the burden on formal support channels and fosters a collaborative environment.
5. **Increased Visibility**: A strong community can enhance your application's visibility. Engaged users are more likely to share their experiences and promote your application through word-of-mouth, social media, and other channels.

2. Building an Engaged User Community

2.1. Creating a Welcoming Environment

1. **Onboarding Experience**: Develop a smooth onboarding process for new users that guides them through key features and functionalities. Consider creating tutorials, guides, or videos to help users get started.
2. **User-Friendly Documentation**: Provide comprehensive and user-friendly documentation that covers installation, configuration, and troubleshooting. Good documentation helps users navigate your application effectively.
3. **Inclusive Language**: Use inclusive and friendly language in your communications, whether in documentation, social media posts, or user interactions. This helps create a welcoming atmosphere for users of all backgrounds.

2.2. Facilitating User Interaction

1. **Discussion Forums**: Create a discussion forum or platform where users can ask questions, share tips, and discuss features. This fosters interaction and builds a sense of community.
2. **Feedback Mechanisms**: Implement feedback mechanisms within the application, such as a feedback form or suggestion box. Encourage users to share their thoughts on features, performance, and usability.
3. **User Events and Webinars**: Organize user events, webinars, or meetups to engage with your community. These events provide

opportunities for networking, learning, and sharing experiences.

3. Encouraging User Feedback and Contributions

3.1. Actively Seek Feedback

1. **Surveys and Polls**: Regularly conduct surveys and polls to gather feedback on specific features or overall satisfaction. Use the insights gained to inform development priorities.
2. **Beta Testing Programs**: Implement beta testing programs that allow users to test new features before they are officially released. Encourage users to provide feedback during the testing phase.
3. **User Interviews**: Conduct one-on-one interviews with users to gather in-depth feedback about their experiences. This qualitative data can provide valuable insights into user needs and pain points.

3.2. Implementing a Contribution Model

1. **Open Source Contributions**: If applicable, encourage users to contribute to the codebase. Provide clear guidelines for contributing, including how to submit pull requests and report issues.
2. **Recognition and Incentives**: Recognize and reward users who contribute to the application, whether through coding, documentation, or community support. Consider offering incentives, such as badges, shout-outs, or exclusive access to new features.
3. **Documentation for Contributors**: Provide thorough documentation for potential contributors, including coding standards, architecture overviews, and setup instructions. This helps new contributors get up to speed quickly.

4. Creating Support Channels

CHAPTER 13: COMMUNITY AND SUPPORT IN APPLICATION DEVELOPMENT

4.1. Establishing Help and Support Resources

1. **Support Documentation**: Create a dedicated support section on your website or application that includes FAQs, troubleshooting guides, and how-to articles.
2. **Knowledge Base**: Consider implementing a knowledge base where users can search for solutions to common issues. This self-service approach empowers users to find answers independently.

4.2. Providing Customer Support

1. **Help Desk Software**: Use help desk software to manage support requests effectively. This enables you to track tickets, monitor response times, and analyze common issues.
2. **Live Chat Support**: Implement live chat support to assist users in real-time. This can enhance the user experience and provide immediate assistance for urgent issues.

5. Leveraging Open Source Development

Open source development is a collaborative approach that encourages community involvement and transparency. Leveraging this model can enhance your application and foster a vibrant community.

5.1. Benefits of Open Source Development

1. **Community Contributions**: Allowing the community to contribute to your codebase increases development speed and innovation. Users with diverse expertise can introduce new features and fix bugs.
2. **Transparency**: Open source projects are transparent, allowing users to see how the application works and contributing to trust and credibility.
3. **Learning Opportunities**: Open source development provides learning opportunities for contributors, allowing them to gain experience and

skills while contributing to a real-world project.

5.2. Managing an Open Source Project

1. **Clear Governance**: Establish clear governance guidelines for your open source project. Define roles, responsibilities, and decision-making processes to ensure smooth collaboration.
2. **Contribution Guidelines**: Provide detailed contribution guidelines that outline how to contribute to the project, including coding standards, issue reporting, and pull request procedures.
3. **Community Engagement**: Engage with your community by acknowledging contributions, providing feedback on pull requests, and facilitating discussions around proposed changes.

6. Utilizing Social Media and Online Platforms

Social media and online platforms can be powerful tools for engaging with your community and promoting your application.

6.1. Building a Social Media Presence

1. **Choose Relevant Platforms**: Identify the social media platforms where your target audience is active (e.g., Twitter, Facebook, LinkedIn) and create profiles for your application.
2. **Share Content Regularly**: Share updates, news, tutorials, and user success stories on your social media channels. Consistent posting keeps your audience engaged and informed.
3. **Engage with Users**: Respond to comments, messages, and mentions on social media. Engaging with your audience builds relationships and fosters a sense of community.

6.2. Utilizing Online Communities

1. **Join Relevant Forums**: Participate in online forums and communities related to your application's domain. Share your expertise, answer questions, and promote your application when appropriate.
2. **Contribute to Q&A Sites**: Contribute to Q&A sites like Stack Overflow by answering questions related to your application. This establishes your credibility and draws attention to your project.
3. **Create a Discord or Slack Channel**: Consider creating a dedicated Discord server or Slack channel for your community. These platforms provide real-time communication and collaboration opportunities.

7. Maintaining a Positive Community Environment

Creating and maintaining a positive community environment is essential for fostering engagement and collaboration.

7.1. Establish Community Guidelines

1. **Define Expectations**: Create clear community guidelines that outline acceptable behavior, communication standards, and the consequences of violations.
2. **Enforce Guidelines Consistently**: Actively monitor community interactions and enforce guidelines consistently. Address any issues or conflicts promptly and transparently.

7.2. Promote Inclusivity and Respect

1. **Encourage Diverse Perspectives**: Foster an inclusive environment that values diverse perspectives and backgrounds. This enriches discussions and drives innovation.
2. **Celebrate Contributions**: Recognize and celebrate the contributions of community members, whether through shout-outs on social media,

newsletters, or community events.

7.3. Foster Collaboration

1. **Collaborative Projects**: Encourage collaborative projects within the community. Create hackathons, coding challenges, or feature sprints to promote teamwork and engagement.
2. **Mentorship Opportunities**: Facilitate mentorship opportunities where experienced developers can guide newcomers. This helps build skills and strengthens community bonds.

Conclusion

In this chapter, we explored the critical role of community and support in the development and success of your full-stack application. We discussed the value of building an engaged user community, encouraging user feedback and contributions, creating effective support channels, leveraging open source development, and utilizing social media for engagement.

Chapter 13: Deployment Strategies and Best Practices for Full-Stack Applications

Introduction

Deployment is a critical phase in the software development lifecycle that involves making your application available for users. For full-stack applications, which typically consist of a backend API (often developed with ASP.NET Core) and a frontend (developed with Angular), deployment can be complex. Proper deployment strategies and best practices are essential for ensuring performance, security, and scalability. This chapter will guide you through various deployment strategies and best practices for your full-stack application.

We will cover the following topics:

1. Understanding Deployment Models
2. Preparing Your Application for Deployment
3. Hosting Options for ASP.NET Core
4. Hosting Options for Angular
5. Continuous Integration and Continuous Deployment (CI/CD)
6. Monitoring and Logging in Production
7. Post-Deployment Best Practices
8. Planning for Future Enhancements

By the end of this chapter, you will have a comprehensive understanding of how to deploy your full-stack application effectively and maintain it in a production environment.

1. Understanding Deployment Models

Deployment models refer to the various environments in which your application can run. Understanding these models is essential for choosing the right approach for your application.

1.1. On-Premises Deployment

In an on-premises deployment, your application is hosted on servers that are physically located in your organization's data center. This model provides complete control over the infrastructure, security, and performance.

- **Advantages**:
- Full control over hardware and software configurations.
- Enhanced security for sensitive data.
- Compliance with regulatory requirements.
- **Disadvantages**:
- High upfront costs for hardware and infrastructure.
- Requires ongoing maintenance and management.
- Limited scalability compared to cloud solutions.

1.2. Cloud Deployment

Cloud deployment involves hosting your application on cloud platforms (e.g., AWS, Azure, Google Cloud). This model offers scalability, flexibility, and reduced management overhead.

- **Advantages**:
- Easy to scale resources based on demand.
- Pay-as-you-go pricing models reduce upfront costs.
- Managed services for databases, storage, and security.
- **Disadvantages**:

CHAPTER 13: DEPLOYMENT STRATEGIES AND BEST PRACTICES FOR...

- Less control over infrastructure.
- Potential security concerns with sensitive data.
- Dependence on the cloud provider's reliability.

1.3. Hybrid Deployment

A hybrid deployment combines on-premises and cloud environments. This model allows organizations to maintain critical applications on-premises while leveraging the cloud for scalability and flexibility.

- **Advantages**:
- Flexibility to choose where to host applications based on needs.
- Ability to utilize cloud resources for peak loads or backups.
- Enhanced security for sensitive data by keeping it on-premises.
- **Disadvantages**:
- Increased complexity in managing two environments.
- Potential integration challenges between on-premises and cloud services.

2. Preparing Your Application for Deployment

Proper preparation is essential to ensure a smooth deployment process. This involves several steps to optimize your application for production.

2.1. Build and Publish Your Application

For both ASP.NET Core and Angular, you need to build and publish your application before deploying it.

1. **ASP.NET Core**: Use the following command to publish your ASP.NET Core application:

```bash
Copy code
dotnet publish -c Release
```

1. This command compiles the application and generates the necessary files in the bin/Release/net5.0/publish directory.
2. **Angular**: For your Angular application, use the Angular CLI to build for production:

```bash
Copy code
ng build --prod
```

1. This command creates a production-ready version of your Angular application in the dist/ folder.

2.2. Environment Configuration

Different environments (development, testing, production) may require different configuration settings. Use environment-specific configuration files for your ASP.NET Core application.

1. **appsettings.json**: Create separate configuration files for different environments, such as appsettings.Development.json and appsettings.Production.json.
2. Example structure:

```json
Copy code
{
  "ConnectionStrings": {
    "DefaultConnection": "Server=your_server;Database=YourDatabase;Trusted_Connection=True;"
  },
  "Jwt": {
```

```
    "Key": "Your_Production_Secret_Key",
    "Issuer": "YourApp",
    "Audience": "YourAppUsers"
  }
}
```

1. **Use Environment Variables**: Use environment variables for sensitive information like database connection strings and API keys. This helps keep sensitive data out of your source code.

3. Hosting Options for ASP.NET Core

When it comes to hosting your ASP.NET Core application, you have several options to choose from. Each hosting environment has its advantages and disadvantages.

3.1. Self-Hosting

ASP.NET Core applications can be self-hosted using Kestrel, which is the default web server included with ASP.NET Core. This is a good option for development or small-scale applications.

1. **Run Kestrel Locally**: You can run your application using Kestrel by executing the following command:

```bash
Copy code
dotnet run
```

1. **Production Considerations**: While self-hosting can be convenient, it is generally recommended to use a reverse proxy server (like Nginx or Apache) in a production environment for better performance and

security.

3.2. Cloud Hosting

1. **Microsoft Azure**: Azure App Service is a popular option for hosting ASP.NET Core applications. It offers a fully managed platform with automatic scaling, continuous deployment, and integrated monitoring.

- **Deploying to Azure**: You can publish your application directly from Visual Studio or use Azure CLI commands.

1. **AWS Elastic Beanstalk**: AWS Elastic Beanstalk is another excellent option for hosting ASP.NET Core applications. It provides a quick and easy way to deploy and manage applications in the AWS cloud.

- **Deploying to Elastic Beanstalk**: You can use the AWS Toolkit for Visual Studio to publish your application directly.

1. **DigitalOcean and Heroku**: Both DigitalOcean and Heroku provide platforms for deploying web applications with minimal setup. They offer different levels of management and scaling options.

4. Hosting Options for Angular

Angular applications are typically served as static files, making them easy to host on various platforms. Here are some popular hosting options for Angular:

4.1. Static File Hosting

1. **GitHub Pages**: GitHub Pages is a simple way to host your Angular application for free. You can publish your application by pushing it to a GitHub repository.
2. **Netlify**: Netlify offers free hosting for static websites and provides

CHAPTER 13: DEPLOYMENT STRATEGIES AND BEST PRACTICES FOR...

features like continuous deployment from GitHub and built-in HTTPS.
3. **Vercel**: Vercel is another excellent option for hosting Angular applications. It provides fast deployments and a user-friendly interface.
4. **2. Cloud Hosting**
5. **Firebase Hosting**: Firebase Hosting is a fast and secure way to host your Angular application. It provides a simple command-line interface for deployment.

- **Deploying to Firebase**: Install the Firebase CLI and initialize your project:

```bash
Copy code
npm install -g firebase-tools
firebase init
firebase deploy
```

1. **AWS S3 and CloudFront**: You can host your Angular application on Amazon S3 and use CloudFront as a CDN to deliver content quickly.

- **Deploying to S3**: Build your Angular application and upload the contents of the dist/ folder to your S3 bucket.

5. Continuous Integration and Continuous Deployment (CI/CD)

Implementing CI/CD pipelines can greatly enhance your deployment process by automating builds, tests, and deployments. This helps ensure that your application is always in a deployable state.

5.1. Setting Up CI/CD Pipelines

1. **Choose a CI/CD Tool**: Popular CI/CD tools include Jenkins, GitHub Actions, GitLab CI/CD, and CircleCI. Each tool has its unique features

and integrations.
2. **Create a CI/CD Pipeline**: A typical CI/CD pipeline includes stages for:

- **Build**: Compile the application and run tests.
- **Test**: Execute automated tests to verify the application's functionality.
- **Deploy**: Deploy the application to the desired environment.

1. **Example GitHub Actions Workflow**: Here's an example of a GitHub Actions workflow for deploying an Angular application:

```yaml
Copy code
name: Deploy Angular App

on:
  push:
    branches:
      - main

jobs:
  build:
    runs-on: ubuntu-latest

    steps:
    - name: Checkout Code
      uses: actions/checkout@v2

    - name: Install Dependencies
      run: npm install

    - name: Build Application
      run: npm run build --prod

    - name: Deploy to Firebase
      run: npm install -g firebase-tools
      run: firebase deploy --token ${{ secrets.FIREBASE_TOKEN }}
```

This workflow builds the Angular application and deploys it to Firebase when code is pushed to the main branch.

5.2. Setting Up Automated Testing

Integrate automated testing in your CI/CD pipeline to ensure that any changes do not break existing functionality. Use testing frameworks like Jasmine and Protractor for Angular, and xUnit or NUnit for ASP.NET Core.

6. Monitoring and Logging in Production

Monitoring and logging are critical for maintaining the health of your application in a production environment. They allow you to track performance, diagnose issues, and ensure that your application runs smoothly.

6.1. Implementing Application Insights

1. **Integrate Application Insights**: To integrate Application Insights into your ASP.NET Core application, install the necessary NuGet package:

```bash
Copy code
Install-Package Microsoft.ApplicationInsights.AspNetCore
```

1. **Configure Application Insights**: In your Startup.cs, configure Application Insights:

```csharp
Copy code
public void ConfigureServices(IServiceCollection services)
{
    services.AddApplicationInsightsTelemetry
(Configuration["ApplicationInsights:
```

```
InstrumentationKey"]);
}
```

1. **Track Custom Events**: Use the Application Insights SDK to track custom events and metrics:

```csharp
Copy code
private readonly TelemetryClient _telemetryClient;

public ProductsController(TelemetryClient telemetryClient)
{
    _telemetryClient = telemetryClient;
}

[HttpGet]
public async Task<ActionResult<Product>> GetProduct(int id)
{
    _telemetryClient.TrackEvent("GetProductCalled", new Dictionary<string, string>
        {
            { "ProductId", id.ToString() }
        });

    var product = await _context.Products.FindAsync(id);
    if (product == null)
    {
        _telemetryClient.TrackEvent("ProductNotFound", new Dictionary<string, string>
            {
                { "ProductId", id.ToString() }
            });
        return NotFound();
    }
```

CHAPTER 13: DEPLOYMENT STRATEGIES AND BEST PRACTICES FOR...

```
    return product;
}
```

6.2. Centralized Logging

1. **Use Serilog for Centralized Logging**: Serilog is a popular logging library that supports structured logging and can send logs to various sinks (e.g., files, databases, cloud services).

   - **Install Serilog**: Install the Serilog NuGet packages:

```bash
Copy code
Install-Package Serilog.AspNetCore
Install-Package Serilog.Sinks.File
```

   - **Configure Serilog**: In your Program.cs, configure Serilog:

```csharp
Copy code
public class Program
{
    public static void Main(string[] args)
    {
        Log.Logger = new LoggerConfiguration()
            .MinimumLevel.Information()
            .WriteTo.File("logs/myapp.txt", rollingInterval: RollingInterval.Day)
            .CreateLogger();

        try
        {
            Log.Information("Starting web host");
```

```
            CreateHostBuilder(args).Build().Run();
        }
        catch (Exception ex)
        {
            Log.Fatal(ex, "Application start-up failed");
        }
        finally
        {
            Log.CloseAndFlush();
        }
    }

    public static IHostBuilder CreateHostBuilder(string[] args) =>
        Host.CreateDefaultBuilder(args)
        .UseSerilog() // Add this line
        .ConfigureWebHostDefaults(webBuilder =>
            {
                webBuilder.UseStartup<Startup>();
            });
}
```

1. **Log Events and Exceptions**: Use Serilog to log important events and exceptions throughout your application:

```csharp
Copy code
[HttpPost]
public async Task<ActionResult<Product>> CreateProduct(Product product)
{
    try
    {
        _context.Products.Add(product);
        await _context.SaveChangesAsync();
        Log.Information("Product created:
```

CHAPTER 13: DEPLOYMENT STRATEGIES AND BEST PRACTICES FOR...

```
{ProductId}", product.Id);
        return CreatedAtAction
(nameof(GetProduct), new
 { id = product.Id }, product);
    }
    catch (Exception ex)
    {
        Log.Error(ex, "Error creating product");
        return StatusCode(500,
"Internal server error");
    }
}
```

7. Post-Deployment Best Practices

Once your application is deployed, it's essential to follow best practices to maintain its performance and reliability.

7.1. Regular Updates and Maintenance

1. **Keep Dependencies Updated**: Regularly check for updates to your libraries and frameworks to ensure you have the latest security patches and features.
2. **Monitor Performance**: Continuously monitor the performance of your application using the tools discussed earlier. Set up alerts for any performance degradation or errors.

7.2. Backup and Recovery Plans

1. **Implement Regular Backups**: Set up automated backups for your database and application files to prevent data loss in case of failure.
2. **Test Recovery Procedures**: Regularly test your backup and recovery procedures to ensure that you can restore your application quickly if necessary.

7.3. User Feedback and Iteration

1. **Collect User Feedback**: Regularly gather feedback from users to understand their experiences and areas for improvement.
2. **Iterate on Features**: Use user feedback to iterate on features and enhance the overall experience of your application.

8. Planning for Future Enhancements

As your application evolves, you will likely want to add new features and make upgrades to improve functionality. Planning for these changes is essential to minimize disruptions and maintain application stability.

8.1. Prioritize Features Based on User Feedback

Use the feedback gathered from users to prioritize new features. Focus on enhancements that align with user needs and have the potential to provide the most significant impact.

1. **Feature Roadmap**: Create a roadmap that outlines planned features and enhancements, including timelines and resource allocation.

8.2. Implement Feature Flags

Feature flags allow you to deploy new features incrementally without exposing them to all users at once. This approach helps you test new features in production and gather feedback before a full rollout.

1. **Using Feature Flags**: Implement feature flags in your application to control which features are visible to users.

```csharp
Copy code
public class FeatureFlags
{
```

```
    public bool NewFeatureEnabled { get; set; }
}
```

1. **Configuring Feature Flags**: Store feature flag configurations in your appsettings.json or an external configuration service.

8.3. Regularly Plan Upgrades

Regularly assess the need for upgrades to your application's frameworks and libraries. Upgrading can provide performance improvements, new features, and security patches.

1. **Create an Upgrade Schedule**: Develop a schedule for regularly reviewing and upgrading dependencies, including Angular, ASP.NET Core, and third-party libraries.
2. **Testing Before Upgrades**: Before implementing upgrades, thoroughly test your application to identify any potential compatibility issues.

Conclusion

In this chapter, we explored various deployment strategies and best practices for your full-stack application. We discussed the importance of understanding deployment models, preparing your application for deployment, and the various hosting options available for both ASP.NET Core and Angular.

Chapter 14: Final Thoughts and the Future of Your Full-Stack Application

Introduction

As we reach the conclusion of this book, it's essential to reflect on the journey of building and deploying a full-stack application using ASP.NET Core and Angular. We have covered a wide range of topics, from foundational concepts to advanced deployment strategies, security best practices, and community engagement. In this chapter, we will summarize the key concepts, discuss the challenges faced in application development, and explore future trends and enhancements that could shape the direction of your application.

We will cover the following topics:
1. Recap of Key Concepts
2. Challenges in Full-Stack Development
3. The Importance of Community and User Engagement
4. Trends in Full-Stack Development
5. Planning for Future Enhancements
6. The Road Ahead

By the end of this chapter, you will have a clear understanding of the full scope of the development process and insights into how to continue improving and evolving your application.

1. Recap of Key Concepts

Throughout this book, we explored various aspects of developing a full-stack application. Here's a recap of the key concepts covered:

1.1. Understanding the Full-Stack Architecture

- **Front-End and Back-End**: The front-end (Angular) interacts with users, while the back-end (ASP.NET Core) handles data processing, business logic, and database interactions. Understanding how these layers communicate is crucial for building a cohesive application.

1.2. MVC Architecture in ASP.NET Core

- **Model-View-Controller (MVC)**: The MVC pattern separates concerns, making applications more maintainable and scalable. We discussed how models represent data, views render the user interface, and controllers manage user interactions.

1.3. Angular Fundamentals

- **Core Concepts**: We delved into Angular's core concepts, such as components, modules, and services, as well as data binding and lifecycle hooks. Understanding these concepts is vital for building dynamic user interfaces.

1.4. Security Best Practices

- **Securing Applications**: We emphasized the importance of security, discussing strategies like HTTPS enforcement, input validation, authentication, and authorization to protect user data and application integrity.

1.5. Deployment Strategies

- **Deployment Models**: We explored various deployment models (on-premises, cloud, and hybrid) and hosting options for both ASP.NET Core and Angular applications. Understanding deployment strategies is essential for making informed decisions about application hosting.

1.6. Continuous Improvement

- **User Feedback and Engagement**: We discussed the value of user feedback and community engagement in driving continuous improvement. Building a supportive community enhances user loyalty and provides valuable insights for future enhancements.

2. Challenges in Full-Stack Development

While the journey of building a full-stack application can be rewarding, it also comes with its challenges. Here are some common challenges faced during development:

2.1. Complexity of Full-Stack Development

Full-stack development involves working with both front-end and back-end technologies, which can be complex. Developers must be proficient in various languages and frameworks, making it essential to stay updated with best practices and trends.

2.2. Integrating Different Technologies

Integrating different technologies (ASP.NET Core for the back end and Angular for the front end) can present challenges, especially regarding communication between the two layers. Ensuring seamless data exchange and managing API calls requires careful planning and execution.

2.3. Security Concerns

With the increasing frequency of cyberattacks, ensuring the security of your application is paramount. Developers must remain vigilant and proactive in identifying and mitigating security risks throughout the development process.

2.4. Performance Optimization

As applications grow, performance optimization becomes critical. Balancing speed, efficiency, and user experience requires ongoing monitoring and tuning of both the back-end and front-end components.

2.5. Keeping Up with Trends

The tech landscape is constantly evolving, with new tools, frameworks, and best practices emerging regularly. Staying informed and adapting to these changes can be challenging but is necessary for maintaining a competitive edge.

3. The Importance of Community and User Engagement

Building a supportive community around your application is essential for its success. Engaging with users fosters loyalty and encourages collaboration, while community feedback drives continuous improvement.

3.1. Cultivating User Loyalty

Engaged users are more likely to remain loyal to your application. By actively listening to user feedback, addressing concerns, and celebrating contributions, you create a positive experience that encourages users to advocate for your application.

3.2. Encouraging Collaboration

A strong community promotes collaboration among users and developers. Encouraging contributions to the codebase, documentation, or user support not only enhances the application but also fosters a sense of ownership among community members.

3.3. Utilizing User Feedback

Feedback from users is invaluable for identifying pain points, prioritizing features, and refining the user experience. Regularly soliciting feedback and acting on it demonstrates that you value your users' input and are committed to improving their experience.

4. Trends in Full-Stack Development

Staying updated with trends in full-stack development can inform your application's future direction. Here are some key trends to consider:

4.1. Microservices Architecture

Microservices architecture is gaining popularity for building scalable applications. By breaking down applications into smaller, independent services, developers can improve flexibility, scalability, and maintainability.

- **Advantages**:
- Independent deployment of services.
- Easier scalability and resource allocation.
- Improved fault isolation and resilience.

4.2. Progressive Web Applications (PWAs)

PWAs combine the best of web and mobile applications, providing a fast, reliable, and engaging user experience. They can be installed on devices and work offline, making them a compelling choice for developers.

- **Benefits**:
- Enhanced performance and responsiveness.
- Offline capabilities improve user experience.
- Access to native device features.

4.3. Serverless Computing

Serverless computing allows developers to build applications without managing the underlying infrastructure. This model enables automatic scaling, reduced operational costs, and simplified deployment processes.

- **Considerations**:
- Choose appropriate serverless frameworks (e.g., AWS Lambda, Azure Functions).
- Understand the billing model based on usage to avoid unexpected costs.

4.4. Artificial Intelligence and Machine Learning Integration

Integrating AI and machine learning capabilities into applications is becoming increasingly common. These technologies enable enhanced user experiences, such as personalized recommendations and intelligent automation.

- **Applications**:
- Use machine learning models to analyze user behavior and improve engagement.
- Implement chatbots for user support and interaction.

5. *Planning for Future Enhancements*

As you look to the future, planning for enhancements is crucial for ensuring your application remains relevant and meets user needs.

5.1. Feature Roadmapping

Develop a feature roadmap that outlines planned enhancements and new features. This roadmap should prioritize user feedback and align with the overall goals of your application.

1. **Identify Key Features**:

- Analyze user feedback to identify frequently requested features.
- Consider the impact of each feature on user experience and engagement.

1. **Timeline and Resource Allocation**:

- Estimate timelines for development and allocate resources accordingly.
- Communicate the roadmap to your community to manage expectations.

5.2. Regular Upgrades

Plan for regular upgrades of your application's frameworks and libraries to benefit from the latest features, performance improvements, and security patches.

1. **Set a Review Schedule**:

- Regularly review dependencies and plan for upgrades on a set schedule (e.g., quarterly).

1. **Testing and Compatibility**:

- Thoroughly test your application after upgrades to identify compatibility issues.

5.3. User Engagement Strategies

Implement strategies to keep users engaged and informed about new features and updates. This can include newsletters, blog posts, and social media updates.

1. **Highlight New Features**:

- Create documentation and tutorials to showcase new features and enhancements.

1. **Solicit Ongoing Feedback**:

- Regularly engage with users to gather feedback on new features and identify areas for improvement.

6. The Road Ahead

The journey of developing and maintaining a full-stack application is ongoing. As technology evolves and user expectations change, it's essential to remain adaptable and proactive in your approach.

6.1. Embrace Continuous Learning

Stay informed about industry trends, best practices, and emerging technologies. Encourage your development team to engage in continuous learning through courses, workshops, and networking opportunities.

6.2. Foster Innovation

Encourage a culture of innovation within your development team. Create opportunities for brainstorming sessions, hackathons, or experimental projects that allow team members to explore new ideas and technologies.

6.3. Maintain User-Centric Focus

Always prioritize user needs and experiences in your development process. Engage with users, gather feedback, and make data-driven decisions to enhance the application continually.

Conclusion

In this chapter, we summarized the key concepts covered throughout the book and discussed the challenges faced in full-stack development. We explored the importance of community and user engagement, trends in full-stack development, and planning for future enhancements.

By implementing the strategies outlined in this book, you will be well-equipped to build and maintain a successful full-stack application that meets user needs and adapts to the ever-changing technology landscape. Remember, the journey of application development is ongoing, and continuous improvement is key to ensuring your application remains relevant and valuable to users.

Chapter 15: Navigating the Future of Full-Stack Development

Introduction

As we conclude this comprehensive exploration of full-stack application development using ASP.NET Core and Angular, it's important to consider the future of this rapidly evolving field. Technology continues to advance at an unprecedented pace, and staying ahead of these changes is crucial for developers and organizations alike. This chapter will examine the future landscape of full-stack development, focusing on emerging technologies, methodologies, and trends that will shape the next generation of applications.

We will cover the following topics:
1. The Evolution of Full-Stack Development
2. Emerging Technologies to Watch
3. Trends in Development Methodologies
4. The Role of DevOps and Automation
5. User Experience and Design Trends
6. The Importance of Security in Future Applications
7. Preparing for a Changing Landscape

By the end of this chapter, you will have a deeper understanding of the trends

CHAPTER 15: NAVIGATING THE FUTURE OF FULL-STACK DEVELOPMENT

and technologies that will impact the future of full-stack development and how to prepare for the changes ahead.

1. The Evolution of Full-Stack Development

1.1. From Monolithic to Microservices

Historically, web applications were often developed as monolithic structures, where the front-end and back-end were tightly coupled. While this approach has its advantages, it can also lead to scalability issues and difficulties in maintenance.

- **Monolithic Architecture**: In a monolithic architecture, all components of the application are interconnected. This makes deployment easier initially, but as the application grows, updates can become complex and time-consuming.
- **Microservices Architecture**: The rise of microservices architecture has changed the landscape of application development. In this approach, applications are broken down into smaller, independent services that can be developed, deployed, and scaled independently.

1.2. The Rise of Full-Stack Frameworks

The emergence of full-stack frameworks has made it easier for developers to build applications that encompass both the front-end and back-end.

- **Full-Stack Frameworks**: Frameworks such as MERN (MongoDB, Express, React, Node.js) and MEAN (MongoDB, Express, Angular, Node.js) provide a cohesive environment for developing full-stack applications. These frameworks streamline development processes by offering integrated tools and libraries.

1.3. The Role of APIs in Full-Stack Development

APIs (Application Programming Interfaces) play a crucial role in modern full-stack development by enabling communication between the front-end and back-end.

- **RESTful APIs**: REST (Representational State Transfer) has become a widely adopted architectural style for building APIs. RESTful APIs allow developers to create stateless interactions between clients and servers, promoting scalability and flexibility.
- **GraphQL**: An emerging alternative to REST, GraphQL allows clients to request only the data they need, reducing over-fetching and under-fetching of data. This flexibility enhances performance and user experience.

2. Emerging Technologies to Watch

As full-stack development continues to evolve, several emerging technologies have the potential to shape the future of application development.

2.1. Progressive Web Applications (PWAs)

Progressive Web Applications combine the best features of web and mobile applications. They provide an app-like experience while being accessible through a web browser.

- **Key Features of PWAs**:
- Offline functionality: PWAs can work offline or on low-quality networks, providing a seamless experience for users.
- App-like experience: PWAs can be installed on a user's device and launched like traditional apps, offering improved engagement.
- Enhanced performance: PWAs are optimized for speed and responsiveness, enhancing user satisfaction.

2.2. Serverless Computing

Serverless computing abstracts away server management, allowing developers to focus on writing code while the cloud provider handles scaling and infrastructure.

- **Benefits of Serverless**:
- Reduced operational costs: Pay only for the compute time you use, rather than maintaining dedicated servers.
- Automatic scaling: Serverless platforms automatically scale based on demand, eliminating concerns about capacity.
- Rapid development: Developers can deploy code quickly without worrying about the underlying infrastructure.

2.3. Low-Code and No-Code Development

Low-code and no-code platforms enable users to create applications with minimal coding expertise, democratizing software development.

- **Key Features**:
- Drag-and-drop interfaces: Users can design applications visually, significantly reducing development time.
- Rapid prototyping: Low-code platforms enable rapid iteration and testing of application ideas, fostering innovation.

2.4. Artificial Intelligence and Machine Learning

Integrating AI and machine learning into applications is becoming increasingly common, enabling developers to create smarter and more responsive applications.

- **Applications of AI/ML**:
- Personalization: AI can analyze user behavior and preferences to deliver

personalized content and recommendations.
- Automation: Machine learning algorithms can automate repetitive tasks, improving efficiency.

3. Trends in Development Methodologies

The methodologies used in software development are evolving, reflecting changes in technology and user needs. Here are some key trends to watch:

3.1. Agile and DevOps

Agile methodologies promote iterative development and collaboration, while DevOps emphasizes the integration of development and operations for continuous delivery.

- **Agile Practices**: Implementing Agile practices, such as Scrum or Kanban, helps teams adapt to changing requirements and improve collaboration.
- **DevOps Culture**: A DevOps culture fosters collaboration between development and operations teams, enhancing communication and streamlining deployment processes.

3.2. Continuous Integration and Continuous Deployment (CI/CD)

CI/CD practices automate the integration and deployment of code changes, enabling teams to deliver new features and updates more frequently and reliably.

- **Benefits of CI/CD**:
- Faster feedback loops: Developers receive immediate feedback on code changes, allowing for quicker resolution of issues.
- Reduced manual errors: Automation minimizes the risk of human error during deployment.
- Increased deployment frequency: Teams can deploy updates more

CHAPTER 15: NAVIGATING THE FUTURE OF FULL-STACK DEVELOPMENT

frequently, improving responsiveness to user feedback.

4. The Role of DevOps and Automation

DevOps and automation are transforming how applications are developed, deployed, and maintained. By adopting these practices, organizations can achieve greater efficiency and reliability.

4.1. Infrastructure as Code (IaC)

Infrastructure as Code (IaC) involves managing infrastructure through code, enabling automated provisioning and management of servers and services.

- **Benefits of IaC:**
- Consistency: IaC ensures that environments are provisioned consistently, reducing discrepancies between development and production environments.
- Version control: Infrastructure configurations can be versioned and managed using the same tools as application code.

4.2. Containerization

Containerization allows developers to package applications and their dependencies into containers, ensuring consistency across different environments.

- **Docker**: Docker is a popular containerization platform that simplifies application deployment and scaling. Containers can run on any machine with Docker installed, enhancing portability.

4.3. Orchestration Tools

Orchestration tools like Kubernetes enable the management of containerized applications across clusters of machines. They automate deployment, scaling, and management of containerized applications.

- **Benefits of Orchestration**:
- Automatic scaling: Orchestration tools can automatically scale applications based on demand, improving resource utilization.
- Self-healing: These tools can automatically restart failed containers, ensuring high availability.

5. User Experience and Design Trends

User experience (UX) and design play a crucial role in the success of applications. Here are some trends to consider:

5.1. Minimalist Design

Minimalist design focuses on simplicity and clarity, emphasizing essential elements while eliminating unnecessary distractions.

- **Benefits of Minimalist Design**:
- Improved usability: Users can easily navigate applications with clear and concise interfaces.
- Faster load times: Simplified designs often result in lighter pages, leading to faster load times.

5.2. Dark Mode

Dark mode has gained popularity in recent years, offering users a visually appealing alternative to traditional light themes. Many applications now provide dark mode options to enhance user experience.

CHAPTER 15: NAVIGATING THE FUTURE OF FULL-STACK DEVELOPMENT

- **Considerations for Dark Mode**:
- Ensure sufficient contrast for readability.
- Allow users to toggle between light and dark modes based on their preferences.

5.3. Micro-Interactions

Micro-interactions are subtle animations or feedback that enhance user engagement. These interactions can guide users through tasks and provide confirmation of actions.

- **Examples**:
- Button hover effects that change color or size.
- Loading indicators that inform users of progress.

6. The Importance of Security in Future Applications

As technology advances, so do security threats. Ensuring the security of applications is crucial for protecting user data and maintaining trust.

6.1. Evolving Threat Landscape

The threat landscape is constantly changing, with new vulnerabilities and attack vectors emerging regularly. Developers must stay informed about potential threats and implement security measures accordingly.

Common Threats:

- **SQL Injection**: Attackers inject malicious SQL code to manipulate databases.
- **Cross-Site Scripting (XSS)**: Attackers inject scripts into web pages viewed by other users.
- **Cross-Site Request Forgery (CSRF)**: Attackers trick users into executing unwanted actions on web applications.

6.2. Security Best Practices

To protect applications from evolving threats, developers should adhere to security best practices:

1. **Input Validation**: Validate and sanitize all user input to prevent injection attacks.
2. **Use HTTPS**: Ensure all communications are encrypted using HTTPS.
3. **Regular Security Audits**: Conduct security audits and penetration testing to identify vulnerabilities.

Conclusion: Charting Your Path in Full-Stack Development

As we conclude this comprehensive guide on full-stack development using ASP.NET Core and Angular, it's essential to reflect on the journey you have undertaken and the skills you've acquired. The world of software development is dynamic, with technologies evolving rapidly and user expectations constantly shifting. In this conclusion, we will summarize the key insights from the book, discuss the importance of continuous learning, and offer guidance on navigating the future of full-stack development.

1. Recap of Key Insights

1.1. Understanding Full-Stack Development

Full-stack development encompasses both front-end and back-end technologies, allowing developers to build complete applications. Understanding how these layers interact is fundamental to creating cohesive, efficient, and user-friendly applications. Throughout this book, you learned about:

- **Architecture**: The MVC (Model-View-Controller) pattern is crucial for organizing your ASP.NET Core backend. This separation of concerns

simplifies development and maintenance.
- **Front-End Frameworks**: Angular is a powerful front-end framework that facilitates the creation of dynamic and responsive user interfaces. Familiarity with its core concepts, such as components, modules, and services, is essential for effective development.

1.2. Security Best Practices

Security is a paramount concern in application development. As threats evolve, so must our defenses. Key security practices discussed include:

- **Input Validation and Sanitization**: Protect your application from injection attacks by validating and sanitizing all user inputs.
- **Authentication and Authorization**: Implement robust authentication mechanisms, such as JWT tokens, to secure your API endpoints and manage user access.
- **Regular Security Audits**: Conduct regular security assessments to identify and mitigate vulnerabilities.

1.3. Deployment Strategies

Deployment is a critical phase in the software development lifecycle. Understanding deployment models and best practices helps ensure a smooth transition from development to production. You explored:

- **Hosting Options**: Various hosting solutions, from self-hosting with Kestrel to cloud platforms like Azure and AWS, offer flexibility and scalability.
- **Continuous Integration and Continuous Deployment (CI/CD)**: Automating the deployment process with CI/CD pipelines improves efficiency and reduces the risk of errors.

CONCLUSION: CHARTING YOUR PATH IN FULL-STACK DEVELOPMENT

1.4. Community and User Engagement

Building a supportive community around your application enhances user loyalty and provides valuable feedback. Engaging with users through:

- **Feedback Mechanisms**: Implementing surveys, interviews, and user testing helps you gather insights into user needs and pain points.
- **Community Support**: Creating forums, discussion groups, and social media channels fosters collaboration and knowledge sharing.

2. The Importance of Continuous Learning

The field of software development is ever-changing, and staying current with emerging technologies, frameworks, and best practices is essential for success. Embracing a mindset of continuous learning will empower you to:

2.1. Adapt to New Technologies

As new tools and frameworks emerge, being adaptable allows you to integrate innovative solutions into your development process. Keeping an eye on industry trends helps you make informed decisions about the technologies you choose to adopt.

2.2. Enhance Your Skills

Engaging in continuous learning opportunities—such as online courses, workshops, and conferences—can help you deepen your expertise in full-stack development and related fields. Consider exploring:

- **Advanced JavaScript**: Understanding modern JavaScript features (ES6 and beyond) will enhance your Angular development.
- **Cloud Computing**: Familiarizing yourself with cloud services and architecture can improve your deployment and scalability strategies.

- **DevOps Practices**: Learning about DevOps principles and tools can streamline your development and deployment processes.

3. Navigating the Future of Full-Stack Development

The future of full-stack development is promising, with numerous trends shaping the landscape. As you move forward, consider the following key trends and technologies that will influence your development journey:

3.1. Embracing Microservices Architecture

Microservices architecture allows developers to build applications as a collection of small, independent services that communicate over APIs. This approach enhances scalability, maintainability, and resilience. As you design new features or overhaul existing components, consider how microservices can benefit your application architecture.

3.2. Leveraging Serverless Computing

Serverless computing abstracts infrastructure management, allowing you to focus solely on application code. By adopting serverless architectures, you can build scalable applications with reduced operational overhead. Familiarize yourself with platforms like AWS Lambda or Azure Functions to explore this paradigm.

3.3. Adopting Progressive Web Applications (PWAs)

Progressive Web Applications combine the best aspects of web and mobile applications, offering enhanced performance and user experiences. By adopting PWA principles, you can create applications that work offline, load quickly, and deliver a seamless experience across devices.

3.4. Integrating AI and Machine Learning

Incorporating AI and machine learning capabilities into your applications can significantly enhance functionality and user experience. Explore machine learning libraries and frameworks to identify opportunities for intelligent features, such as personalized recommendations or automated decision-making.

4. Preparing for Challenges Ahead

As you navigate the future of full-stack development, be prepared to face challenges and uncertainties. Here are some strategies to help you stay resilient:

4.1. Cultivate a Growth Mindset

Adopting a growth mindset will empower you to embrace challenges as opportunities for growth. Recognize that setbacks and failures are part of the learning process, and approach them with a willingness to learn and adapt.

4.2. Build a Strong Network

Engaging with other developers and industry professionals can provide valuable insights, support, and collaboration opportunities. Attend local meetups, join online communities, and connect with peers through social media platforms.

4.3. Stay Informed

Regularly consume content related to full-stack development, including blogs, podcasts, and webinars. Staying informed about industry trends and best practices will help you make informed decisions and stay competitive.

Conclusion: Your Journey Ahead

In closing, the journey of full-stack development is one of continuous learning, adaptation, and improvement. By applying the concepts and practices discussed in this book, you are well-equipped to build robust, secure, and user-centric applications. Embrace the challenges and opportunities that lie ahead, and remain committed to enhancing your skills and knowledge.

Remember, the tech landscape will continue to evolve, presenting new possibilities and challenges. Approach each phase of development with curiosity and a willingness to adapt, and your applications will thrive in the ever-changing world of technology.

www.ingramcontent.com/pod-product-compliance
Lightning Source LLC
Chambersburg PA
CBHW071020240526
45469CB00006BD/2009